Angel Mariah

The
MARK
Of The
FEASTS!

Pearly Gates Publishing, LLC, Houston, Texas (USA)

The Mark of the Feasts!

The Mark of the Feasts

Copyright © 2017
Angel Mariah

All Rights Reserved.
No portion of this publication may be reproduced, stored in any electronic system, or transmitted in any form or by any means (electronic, mechanical, photocopy, recording, or otherwise) without written permission from the publisher. Brief quotations may be used in literary reviews.

Scripture references are used with permission from Zondervan via Biblegateway.com.

ISBN 13: 978-1-945117-90-9

Library of Congress Control Number: 2017956113

For information and bulk ordering, contact:
Pearly Gates Publishing, LLC
Angela R. Edwards, CEO
P.O. Box 62287
Houston, TX 77205
BestSeller@PearlyGatesPublishing.com

Angel Mariah

*"Whom the heaven must receive until the time of **"Restoration of all Things"** which God hath spoken by the mouth of all His holy prophets since the world began"* (Acts 3:21).

The Mark of the Feasts!

> **Deuteronomy 6:4**
>
> שְׁמַע יִשְׂרָאֵל יְיָ אֱלֹהֵינוּ יְיָ אֶחָד:
>
> *Sh'ma Yisrael Adonai Elohaynu Adonai Echad.*
>
> **Hear, Israel, the Lord is our God,
> the Lord is ONE...**

Angel Mariah

> "'*Go through the midst of the city*
> *through the midst of Jer***USA***lem,*
> *and set a* **mark** *upon the foreheads of the men*
> *that sigh and that cry for all the abominations*
> *that be done in the midst thereof.*'
> *And to the others He said in mine hearing,*
> '*Go ye after him through the city, and smite:*
> *let not your eye spare, neither have ye pity:*
> *Slay utterly old and young, both maids*
> *and little children, and women:*
> *but come not near any man upon whom*
> *is the* **mark***; and begin at my sanctuary.*'
> *Then they began at the ancient men*
> *which were before the house.*"
>
> **Ezekiel 9:4-6**

The Mark of the Feasts!

*"Be not forgetful to entertain strangers:
for thereby some have entertained angels unawares."*
Hebrews 13:2

Angel Mariah

A Prayer

Dear God, help us to find our way home, the way which we went. Turn again our captivity.

Help us to understand that we have not known our true identity as Your Chosen people because we were blinded for a season and scattered among the heathen.

Join us together, Ephraim and Judah, into one stick that we may become **ONE** in Your hand. Cause Your breath to enter into our dry bones that we may live and stand upon our feet; an exceeding great army.

Lead us as we seek to build the old waste places for both Ephraim and Judah. Open our graves and cause us to come up into our own land of Israel, *Your Promised Land!*

Empower us to set up waymarks; to repair the breach; to restore all the things that bring glory and honor to Your Name. Cause us to be the true virgins spoken of by Your prophets of old.

Help us also to have Holy Feasts that prepare us to meet You face to face in all Your glory.

The Mark of the Feasts!

Put our feet on the ancient paths that we might stand in the gap and return to You in righteousness. Take away the *stony heart* out of our flesh and give us a heart of flesh.

Put Your laws in our inward parts and write them on our hearts; put Your Holy Spirit within us and cause us to walk in Your statutes, that we may keep Your judgments and do them…so shall we be Your people and so shall You be our God!

Let the whole earth be filled with Your glory; may we cry out with a loud voice, "HOLY, HOLY, HOLY; worthy is the Lamb that was slain to receive power, and riches, and wisdom, and strength, and honor, and glory, and blessing".

May every creature which is in Heaven, and on the earth, and under the earth, and such as are in the sea, and all that are in them, say, *"Blessing, and honor, and glory, and power, be unto Him that sitteth upon the throne, and unto the Lamb forever and ever"*.

Even so, come Yeshua HaMashiach!

Angel Mariah

DEDICATION

This book is dedicated to my Mother,

THE ONE & ONLY

Mae Otis Henton.

I Love You, Mommy Dearest!

The Mark of the Feasts!

ACKNOWLEDGEMENT

It's been often said that *"The Jews kept the Book"* and *"The Book kept the Jews"*. **Mark of the Feasts** is truly an offspring of that relationship!

For more than 25 years, I have been on a personal spiritual pilgrimage towards home to learn, study, teach, and live the ways found in this sacred book known as the Bible, **Torah**.

So, it is with humble gratitude that I thank **all** of you —

"Keepers of the Book"!

Shomer Doltot Yisrael!
שומר דלתות ישראל

INTRODUCTION

*"To everything there is a season,
and a time to every purpose under the Heaven."*
(Ecclesiastes 3:1)

How much would you know about the history of America's independence without the celebration of the 4th of July, fireworks, parades, barbeques, fairs, picnics, music, concerts, and family reunions? Think about it. Would you know **anything** about the American Revolution, the 13 colonies, or the Declaration of Independence?

In similar fashion, God gave us instructions to learn about **His** history through Mo'edims — the Hebrew word for "feasts", "appointed times", or "divine appointments".

Each of these seven Feasts are messages and they come in clusters: four in the Spring and three in the Fall. The Spring Feasts are a picture of the Messiah's first coming. He was sacrificed on Passover, buried on Unleavened Bread, and rose on First Fruits.

The Fall Feasts are a picture of the Messiah's second coming and the beginning of the "Tikkiun Olam" — the world to

The Mark of the Feasts!

come! Paul wrote to the church in Colossians 2:16-17 that the Holy Days are a *"shadow of things to come"*.

These Holy Feast Days are blueprints for the plan of God and each one teaches us about our wonderful relationship with Him.

The Hebrew word for feast or festival is "mo'ed", which means we have fixed or appointed times to meet with God. Honoring these Holy Days will help you to:

- Better understand Torah and God's instructions.
- Discover the original Hebrew roots of Christianity.
- Understand God's plan for our lives here on earth.
- More deeply understand the life and purpose of the Messiah's mission.
- Get greater insights into God's prophetic times and seasons.
- Get a clearer picture of God's lunar calendar according to the heavens.
- Learn hands-on object lessons to teach the children — young and old.
- Institute Godly traditions and create memories your children will cherish.

Angel Mariah

To fully comprehend our Christian faith, we must know about our fascinating Hebrew heritage. We study a Hebrew book, written by Hebrews; we serve a Hebrew Messiah who had Hebrew disciples; we desire to follow the first century church—which was first predominantly Hebrew; and through the Messiah death, burial, and resurrection, we are grafted into a Hebrew family! *It only makes sense to study the Hebrew culture!* This is a refreshing, new, and exciting way to view and study the Torah.

Today, many are waking to the realization of how important it is to understand our Hebraic roots and spiritual heritage. There is a quiet revival as people from around the world are returning to honor God in the same manner as in the days of old.

> *"And they that shall be of thee shall build the old waste places:*
> *thou shalt raise up the foundations of many generations;*
> *and thou shalt be called, The Repairer of the Breach,*
> *The Restorer of Paths to dwell in."*
> (Isaiah 58:12)

TABLE OF CONTENTS

A Prayer	x
DEDICATION	xii
ACKNOWLEDGEMENT	xiii
INTRODUCTION	xiv
Overview of the 7 Feasts - Holy Days	2
7 Feasts Master List	10
7 Feasts Days - Chart of Holy Days	12
Overview of the Spring Feasts	13
Counting of the Omer	14
Overview of The Omer & Interlude	15
The Interlude of the Spring Feasts	16
Counting of the Omer - Details	17
Blessing for Counting of the Omer	20
Feasts of Passover	23
Feasts of Unleavened Bread	29
Feasts of First Fruits	34
Feasts of Weeks - Pentecost	39
The Interlude	46
Overview of the Fall Feasts	48
Overview of Elul, Teshuvah, and Tashlich	50
The 40-Day Period of Teshuvah	54
Why 40 Days?	55
The Tradition of Tashlich	63

Feasts of Trumpets -- 67
Jewish Customs of Trumpets -- 71
The Civil and Religious Calendars --- 75
Four Themes of Trumpets --- 77
Feasts Day of Atonement -- 88
Feasts of Tabernacles -- 99
How to Build a Sukkah -- 106
Sukkot - Messiah's Birth --- 110
Feasts of Dedication - Hanukkah --- 116
CONCLUSION -- 124
ABOUT THE AUTHOR -- 126
BIBLIOGRAPHY -- 128
NOTES: -- 130

The Mark of the Feasts!

"These are the LORD'S appointed Feasts!"
Leviticus Chapter 23

Angel Mariah

Overview of the 7 Feasts - Holy Days
(As Recorded in Leviticus Chapter 23)

Overview

People all over the planet observe various holidays according to their culture or country. These are often in memory or celebration of significant political or religious events. Such celebrations can be as simple as honoring birth dates of national heroes or as diverse as the observance of religious beliefs and superstitions. Worldwide, thousands of different holidays are observed annually.

In marked contrast, God instituted seven holidays to be observed. While it is not entirely inappropriate for men to observe and establish special holiday celebrations, their social acceptance cannot be compared with the significance and importance of the Seven Holy Days commanded by God to be annually observed by His people forever!

These holidays are known by many different titles: **Holy Days, Sabbaths, Feast Days, Holy Convocations, Holy Rehearsals, and Holy Festivals.**

Most Christians, church leaders included, know little about the *"Feasts of the Lord"*. Historically, the church has often

The Mark of the Feasts!

fought bitterly against anyone honoring what they mistakenly call the "Jewish Feasts". Even today, many in the churches know very little about them.

These **Seven Feasts** are discussed throughout the entire Bible, in both the 1st and 2nd Testaments. However, it is only in one place—Leviticus 23—where all seven Feast Days are listed in chronological sequence. There, they are called the "Feasts of the Lord", which indicates that these Feast Days are God's days. They were instituted "by Him" and they belong "to Him" and only on "His terms" and at "His invitation" can men participate in them and enter into their many benefits.

In Leviticus 23:1-2,4, it is written:
*"And the **LORD** spake unto Moses saying, "Speak unto the children of Israel, and say unto them, 'Concerning the **FEASTS** of the **LORD**, which you shall proclaim to be holy convocations [which means "rehearsals"] even these are **MY FEASTS**.*
*These are the **FEASTS** of the **LORD**,*
even holy convocations which you shall proclaim in the seasons ["mo'ed" — "an exact time, a set time, or an appointed time]'."

These Seven Feasts are thus **"Divine Appointments"** with God!

Notice that Leviticus 23:1-2, 4 says that these are the "**FEASTS** of the **LORD**". It does **not** say that these are the "Feasts of the *JEWS*".

Note that the Feasts *absolutely* cannot be kept exactly as outlined in the Torah; specific sacrifices were required at these Feasts. Although Colossians 2:14 says the sacrifices were taken away at the cross with the true sacrifice of Yeshua, none of the actual Feast Days have been abolished.

The Hebrew word for 'Feasts' is mo'edim, which means appointed times. The idea is that the sequence and timing of each of these Feasts have been carefully appointed by God and are based on "*His time*" according to the lunar clock. Each is an integral part of the comprehensive whole.

Collectively, they tell a story and are intended to be times of meetings between God and man for "holy purposes". And, since they are "*appointments*" or "*appointed times*" for "*holy purposes*", they carry with them great sacredness and solemnity.

These Feasts are divided into three primary categories that outline God's plan of redemption. They portray a broad three-phase plan for our lives; personal Redemption, filling of the Holy Spirit, and Restoration. Each is a time of physical

The Mark of the Feasts!

events that typify spiritual experiences. They have to do with physical harvests and offerings that portray spiritual harvests and offerings.

The Feasts Days come in clusters. The first three are the Spring Feasts: *Passover, Unleavened Bread,* and *First of the First Fruits*. These occur in the Spring during an eight-day period and they are often collectively called "Passover".

The next Feast Day is the late Spring Feasts called *Shavuot*. Shavuot comes by itself, 50 days after the waving of the First Fruits. Many know this early Summer Feast by its Greek name, Pentecost, which means '50'. It is also sometimes called the "Feast of Weeks" (Exodus 34:22).

The next collection of Feasts are the three Fall Feasts. They are the **Day of Blowing of Trumpets, Day of Atonement,** and **Tabernacles**. These latter Feasts cover a 21-day period and are collectively referred to as the **"Fall Feasts"**, or more often as **"Tabernacles"**.

The three Fall Feasts were decreed to be "Solemn Feasts"— (Exodus 23:14-17; Deuteronomy 16:16; 2 Chronicles 8:13; cf. Exodus 34:22-23) — during which time all Israelite males were obligated to go on pilgrimage to Jerusalem to "*appear before the Lord*" (Deuteronomy 16:16).

These three Pilgrimage Feasts are **Passover/Unleavened Bread**, **Shavuot**, and **Tabernacles**. In keeping this commandment, the Messiah journeyed to Jerusalem for each pilgrim feast.

Two of the appointed Feasts have two Sabbath days within them. These double Feasts are Unleavened Bread and the Feast of Booths (or Tabernacles). We are commanded to do no work on the first and last days of both of these Feasts, as they are designated Sabbaths of God.

The principle gift found in the Feasts is that they give us a sweet taste of God and provide us with times to gather together with His people. He gives us these special seasons so we can come together and learn to fulfill the two great commandments: to love God with all our hearts, with all our souls, and with all our strength, and to love our neighbor as ourselves (Matthew 22:36-40).

These Feasts also give us an excellent opportunity to convey to our children the very thing for which Abraham was honored. The Father said of Abraham, "*I have chosen him, so that

The Mark of the Feasts!

he may command his children and his household after him to keep the way of GOD by doing righteousness and justice" (Genesis 18:19).

When we honor the Feasts, our quiet actions speak loudly to our family and friends about our faith. They show our obedience to God, and they especially portray the truth that He blesses and provides for obedience.

Many of the returning children who were scattered among the heathens are now hearing God's whisper in their ears. "Ask for the ancient paths, where the good way is, and walk in it; and you will find rest for your souls" (Jeremiah 6:16). *"Set up for yourself road marks, place for yourself guideposts; direct your mind to the highway, the way by which you went"* (Jeremiah 31:21).

Undoubtedly, there is *NOT* a theme or subject to which a man can give his attention or time that is loftier or more important than the **7 Feasts of the Lord**. Even the number of Feasts Days is significant; the number '7' is the Biblical number for perfection and completion.

Feasts Days always begin at sundown when the new day begins, as commanded in the Torah beginning at creation.

For most of the world, a day is reckoned based on the Roman Gregorian calendar reckoning of time which begins a new day at midnight. However, in marked contrast, all of God's days begins at sundown and continue until the next sundown.

Six times in Genesis 1, the Lord spoke of the day as consisting of "the evening and the morning" (Genesis 1:5, 8, 13, 19, 23, 31). The order of the day was consistent: first the evening (night hours following sunset), then the morning (daylight hours ending at sundown).

Since a major emphasis of **RESTORATION** is to restore and teach the significance of the foundational Biblical Feasts to Bible-believing Christians who have accepted Yeshua as the Messiah, this book stresses why *EVERY* Christian should be celebrating the **"Feasts of the Lord"** every year, every time, just like God commanded. *"For I am the LORD. I change not!"* (Malachi 3:6).

Isaiah 66:23 says, *"And it shall come to pass, that from one new moon to another, and from one Sabbath to another, shall all flesh come to worship before Me, says the LORD"*.

The Mark of the Feasts!

Learn about these **"Feasts of the Lord"** and their importance. They reveal both the 1st and 2nd coming of Yeshua, as well as our personal relationship with God.

THESE ARE the FEASTS of the LORD!
(Leviticus 23:4)

7 Feasts Master List
Holy Days of the Lord - GOD
7 annual Feasts or Festivals
Leviticus Chapter 23
(Comes in clusters)

Spring Feasts: *(Redemption, Sanctification, Resurrection)*

- Three Feasts
- 8-day period

   1st = **Passover (Pesach)** (one of the 3 pilgrimage feasts)

   2nd = **Feast of Unleavened Bread (Matzah)**

   3rd = **First Fruits (Bikkirum)**

Latter Spring Feasts: *(Filling of the Holy Spirit)*

- One Feast (one of the three pilgrimage feasts)
- 50 days later

   4th = **Pentecost (Shavuot)** — sometimes called Feast of Weeks

"And the Lord spoke unto Moses, saying,
'Speak unto the children of Israel, and say unto them,
"Concerning the Feasts of the Lord, which ye shall proclaim
to be Holy Convocations, even these are My Feasts.
Six days shall work be done: but the seventh day is the Sabbath
of rest, an Holy Convocation; ye shall do no work therein: it is the
Sabbath of the Lord in all your dwellings'".
Leviticus 23:1-3

The Mark of the Feasts!

Fall Feasts: *(Restoration)*
- Three Feasts
- 21-day period

    1st = **Trumpets (Yom Teruah)** — Blowing Shofars & Rosh Hashana

    2nd = **Day of Atonement (Yom Kippur)** — Holiest Day of the Year

    3rd = **Tabernacles (Sukkot)** — Feasts of Booths (one of the three pilgrimage feasts)

Other Feasts *(Festivals)*:
- **Teshuvah** — (40 days of Repentance and Returning)
- **Rosh Hashanah** - The New Year
- **Hanukkah** (Festival of Lights) — (Festival of Dedication)
- **Purim** — (Feasts of Esther) (Feasts of Lots)
- **Rosh Chodesh** — New Moon

"Then Jonathan said to David, Tomorrow is the new moon: and thou shalt be missed, because thy seat will be empty."
(1 Samuel 20:18)

Angel Mariah

7 Feasts Days - Chart of Holy Days
7 annual Feasts or Festivals
Leviticus Chapter 23

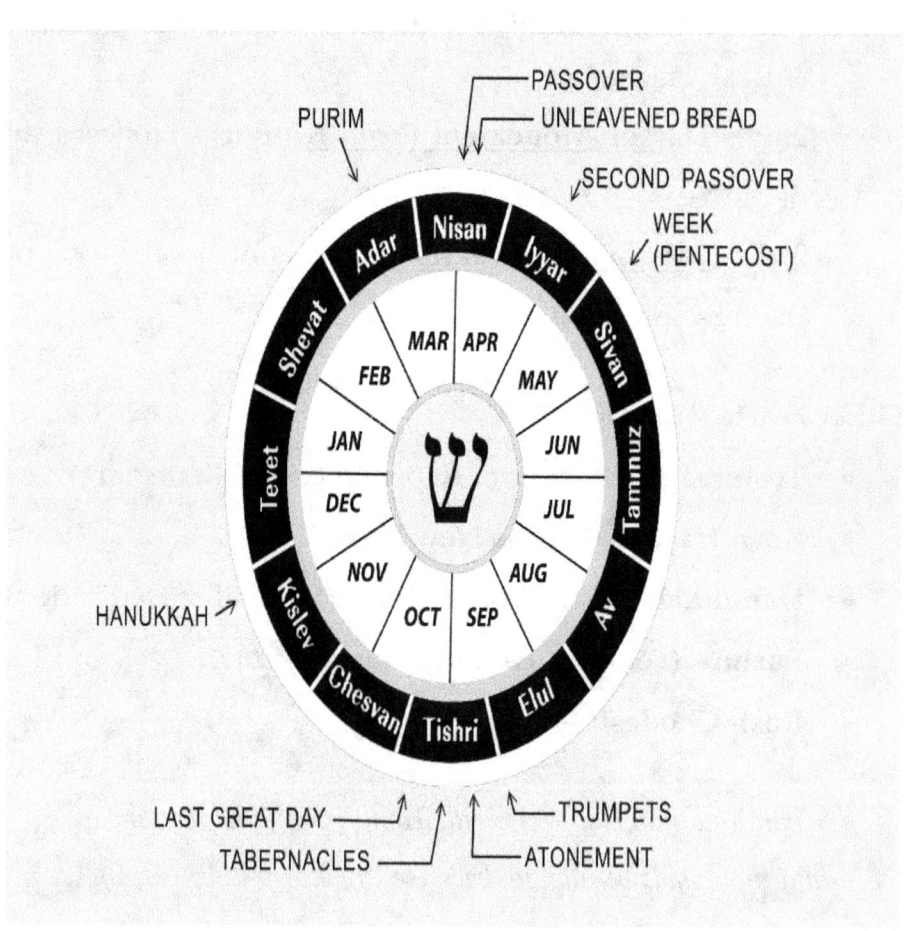

The Mark of the Feasts!

Overview of the Spring Feasts
(A Cluster of Four)

- Four of the seven Feast Days occur in the early and later Spring of the year.
- They typify that all prophecies have been fulfilled in the Messiah.
- In that sense, one can look back and examine them because they are history. They occurred almost 2,000 years ago.
- Their spiritual benefits continue forward to this very day.

Spring Feasts: (Redemption, Sanctification, Resurrection)

- Three Feasts over an eight-day period

    1st = Passover (Pesach) (one of the three pilgrimage feasts)
    2nd = Feast of Unleavened Bread (Matzah)
    3rd = First Fruits (Bikkirum)

Counting of the Omer
(Hebrew - Sefirat Ha'Omer)

- Counting of the Omer is a verbal counting of 49 days between the Feasts of Passover and Shavuot—for a total of 50 days!

Latter Spring Feasts: (Filling of the Holy Spirit)
- One Feast - 50 days later

    4th = Pentecost (Shavuot)—sometimes called Feast of Weeks (one of the three pilgrimage feasts)

The Interlude
Of the Spring Feasts

This is a period—

a gap between the Spring and Fall Holy Feasts!

The Mark of the Feasts!

Overview of The Omer & Interlude
Counting of the Omer
(Hebrew - Sefirat Ha'Omer)

"And count for yourselves from the day after the Shabbat (Feast of Unleavened Bread) from the day you brought the Omer of the wave offering, seven Sabbaths shall be complete. Even to the day after the seventh Sabbath counted are fifty days (50 days) and you shall offer a new grain offering to God"
(Leviticus 23:15-16).

- Counting of the Omer or Sefirat Ha'Omer is a verbal counting of each of the 49 days between the Holy Days of Passover and Shavuot—a total of 50 days.

- This derives from the Torah commandment to count 49 days beginning from the day on which the Omer, a sacrifice containing an Omer-measure of barley, was offered in the Temple in Jerusalem, up until the day before an offering of wheat was brought to the Temple on Shavuot (Pentecost).

- The Counting of the Omer begins on the second day of Passover and ends the day before the holiday of Shavuot, the "50th day".

The Interlude of the Spring Feasts
(The period of time – the gap between the Spring and Fall Holy Feasts)

- There is a gap of time during the long Summer months in which there are no Biblical Holy Days.
- This gap comes immediately following the final Spring Feasts of Shavuot.
- The crops will grow during the Summer months until the arrival of the Fall holidays that speak of events just prior to the second coming of the Messiah.

The Mark of the Feasts!

Counting of the Omer - Details

"Count for yourselves from the day after the Sabbath, from the day you brought the Omer of the wave offering, seven Sabbaths shall be complete. Even to the day after the seventh Sabbath counted are fifty days and you shall offer a new grain offering to GOD."
(Leviticus 23:15-16)

- Counting of the Omer (or Sefirat Ha'Omer) is a verbal counting of each of the 49 days between the Feast of Passover and Shavuot.
- This comes from the Torah commandment to count 49 days beginning from the day on which the Omer, a sacrifice containing an Omer-measure of barley, was offered in the Temple in Jerusalem, up until the day before an offering of wheat was brought to the Temple on Shavuot.
- The Counting of the Omer begins on the second day of Passover and ends the day before the holiday of Shavuot, the '50th day'.
- The Omer is counted each evening after sundown.
- The idea of counting each day represents spiritual preparation and anticipation for the giving of the Torah, which was given by God on Mount Sinai at the

beginning of the month of Sivan, around the same time as Shavuot.

- The Israelites were freed from Egypt at Passover in order to receive the Torah at Sinai, an event which is now celebrated on Shavuot. Thus, the Counting of the Omer demonstrates how much a person desires to accept the Torah in his life.

- This was the reason for the redemption and exodus from Egypt—to receive the Torah at Sinai. Therefore, we are commanded to count from Passover until Shavuot to display our excitement and anticipation towards the Day of the Giving of the Torah.

- *"When you take the people out of Egypt,"* said God to Moses when He revealed Himself to him in a burning bush at the foot of Mount Sinai, *"You shall serve God on this mountain."* It took seven weeks to reach the mountain.

- The people of Israel departed Egypt on the 15th of Nissan (the first day of Passover); on the 6th of Sivan, celebrated ever since as the Festival of Shavuot, they assembled at the foot of Mount Sinai and received the Torah from God.

- The Kabbalists (Jewish mysticism) explain that the 49 days that connect Passover with Shavuot correspond to the 49 drives and traits of the human heart.

The Mark of the Feasts!

- Kabbalists say…"Each year, we retrace this inner journey with our Counting of the Omer". Beginning on the second night of Passover, we count the days and weeks: "Today is one day to the Omer"; "Today is two days to the Omer", "Today is seven days, which is one week to the Omer"; and so on, until "Today is 49 days, which are seven weeks to the Omer".
- Shavuot, the "Festival of Weeks", is the product of this count, driven by the miracles and revelations of the Exodus but achieved by a methodical, 49-step process of self-refinement within the human soul.

Angel Mariah

Blessing for Counting of the Omer
(The 50 Days)

Traditional households anticipate Shavuot by Counting the Omer each and every day from the '7th day Sabbath' of Passover, until the 50th day when Shavuot arrives.

Omer means "sheaf" in Hebrew, like a sheaf of wheat; it's also an allegory for a man standing to worship God. Many American households let 'Counting the Omer' and Shavuot, which literally means 'weeks', pass without much notice because they don't know how to celebrate this wonderful holiday.

Here is a blessing to repeat each day to accomplish this commandment given in Leviticus 23:15-16:

"And ye shall count unto you from the morrow after the Sabbath, from the day that ye brought the sheaf of the waving; seven weeks shall there be complete; even unto the morrow after the seventh week shall ye number fifty days; and ye shall present a new meal-offering unto the LORD."

"Blessed are You LORD our God, King of the Universe who has sanctified us with Your commandments and commanded us

The Mark of the Feasts!

concerning the Counting of the Omer. Today is the (1st-50th) day of the Counting of the Omer."

"Blessed are You, O Lord our God, King of the Universe, who has sanctified us by Your commandments and commanded us to be a light unto the nations and given us Yeshua our Messiah, the Light of the World."

Read the 67th Psalm daily after the above prayers:

"God be merciful to us and bless us. And cause His face to shine upon us. That Your way may be known on earth, Your salvation among all nations. Let the nations praise You, O God;
Let all the nations praise You. Oh, let the nations be glad and sing for joy. For You shall judge the people righteously, and govern the nations on earth. Let the nations Praise You, O God;
Let all the nations praise You. Then the earth shall yield her increase; God, our own God, shall bless us. God shall bless us, and all the ends of the earth shall fear Him."

BA-RUCH A-TAH ADO-NAI E-LO-HE-NU ME-LECH HA-OLAM ASHER KID-E-SHA-NU BE-MITZ-VO-TAV VETZI-VA-NU AL SEFI-RAT HA-OMER.

"Blessed are You LORD our God, King of the Universe who has sanctified us with His commandments and commanded us concerning the Counting of the Omer."

Angel Mariah

"These are the LORD's appointed feasts…you are to proclaim at their appointed times…" "The LORD'S Passover begins at twilight on the fourteenth day of the first month."
Leviticus 23: 4, 5

The Mark of the Feasts!

Feasts of Passover
(1st of the Four Spring Feasts)
Hebrew: Pesach (Pay-sahk)
Leviticus 23:4-5 / Exodus 12:1-4

Specific Notes:

- 1st of the Spring Feasts.
- Considered the 'Foundational Feast'; the six Feasts that follow are built on it.
- Occurs in the Spring of the year.
- Occurs on the 14th day of the Hebrew month of Nisan, which typically falls in March or April of the Gregorian calendar.
- Occurs in the middle of the month during the time of the light of the full moon.
- Passover is a Spring festival, so it typically begins on the night of a full moon after the northern vernal equinox.
- It is NOT a Sabbath but a work day.
- Commemorates God's deliverance of Israel out of Egypt and means to "pass over".
- Includes a meal called "The Seder" (SAY-der) which means "order" in Hebrew.

- One of the three triad of pilgrimage Feasts when all males were required to go to Jerusalem to "appear before the Lord" (Deuteronomy 16:16).

Details:
- Passover is an excellent time to dedicate our homes to the God of Israel. Just as our forefathers painted the blood of the lamb on the doorposts of their homes, we need to envision our entire home being covered by the Blood of Yeshua, the Blood that protects from all evil. You can begin your home dedication by affixing a mezuzah to your doorposts. Then you have a celebration of the Passover Sedar meal.
- The Lord sent Moses to lead the children of Israel from Egypt to the Promised Land. When confronted by Moses, at first Pharaoh refused to let the people go. After sending nine plagues, the Lord said the firstborn males of every house would die unless the doorframe of that house was covered with the blood of a perfect lamb. That night, the Lord "passed over" the homes with the blood on the doorframes. The tenth plague brought death to the firstborn sons of Egypt, even taking the life of Pharaoh's own son. Finally, Pharaoh let the children of Israel go and Passover was to be a lasting ordinance for

generations to come. In Leviticus 23, the Lord said that on the 14th day of the first month (of the Religious New Year), the Lord's Passover was to begin.

- Yeshua at the Passover meal with His disciples, saying that He had eagerly desired to eat this meal with them before He suffered and that He would not eat it again until the Kingdom of God comes (Luke 22:7-16). After the Passover meal, they sang a hymn and went to the Mount of Olives (Matthew 26:30). The hymn sung during Passover is the Hallel which includes Psalm 118:22: *"The stone that the builders rejected has become the cornerstone"* (Matthew 21:42; 1 Peter 2:7).

- Yeshua was crucified on Passover Day, a full moon, as *"the Lamb of God who takes away the sin of the world"* (John 1:29).

- The Christian churches commemorate the Lord's Last Supper as a remembrance of His sacrifice as the perfect Passover Lamb and the fulfillment of the new covenant between God and man (Luke 22:20; 1 Corinthians 5:7; Ephesians 2:11-13). The Hebrew prophet Isaiah also spoke of the sufferings and sacrifice of the Messiah, and how that sacrifice would be the ultimate atonement for the sins of God's people (Isaiah 53).

- Passover carries a powerful significance for us today. This holiday forms the primary background for understanding the events of the Upper Room, the symbolism of the Lord's Last Supper, and the meaning of His death.

Significant Facts:
- Yeshua's parents traveled to Jerusalem yearly to celebrate Passover. At age 12, He went with them (Luke 2:41-50).
- Passover lamb must be a perfect male without spot or blemish (Exodus 12:5).
- The cup of the Lord's Supper is the third cup of the Passover Seder, the Cup of Redemption. The bread of the Lord's Supper is the Afikomen. It is the matzah that is broken, hidden, found, bought for a price, and then eaten to end the meal.
- Afikomen means "I came" in Greek.
- A hymn is usually sung at the end of the Passover service, as was the case with Yeshua and His disciples (Matthew 26:30).
- Yeshua and His followers will observe Passover in the new Kingdom. In Luke 22:18, Yeshua told us that He

would drink again of the *"FRUIT OF THE VINE"* (the cup of Passover) when He returns.

- When we celebrate Passover, we are to view it as God personally redeeming us. In Exodus 13:8, it is written: *"And you shall tell your son in that day, saying, this is done because of what the LORD DID for ME when I came forth out of Egypt"*.

- This is what the Apostle Paul was trying to communicate in 1 Corinthians 10:1, as it is written: *"Moreover, brethren, I would not that you should be ignorant how that **ALL OUR** fathers were under the cloud and **ALL** passed through the sea..."*

- Passover in 1st Testament verses: Exodus 12; Numbers 9; 28:16-25; 2 Chronicles 35:1-19; Ezra 6:19; Ezekiel 45:21.

- Passover in 2nd Testament verses: Matthew 26; Mark 14; Luke 22; John 6:4; 11; 13; 19; 1 Corinthians 5:7.

Angel Mariah

"These are the LORD's appointed feasts...you are to proclaim at their appointed times...The LORD's Passover begins at twilight on the fourteenth day of the first month. On the fifteenth day of that month the LORD's Festival of Unleavened Bread begins; for seven days you must eat bread made without yeast. On the first day hold a sacred assembly and do no regular work. For seven days present a food offering to the LORD. And on the seventh day hold a sacred assembly and do no regular work."
Leviticus 23: 4, 5-8

The Mark of the Feasts!

Feasts of Unleavened Bread

2nd of the Spring Feasts
Hebrew: Hag HaMatzot (Hawg Hah MAHT zot)
Exodus 12:15-20 / Leviticus 23:6-8
Deuteronomy 6:1-8

General Facts:

- The 2nd of the cluster of four Spring Feasts observed in the early Spring (March/April).
- Begins on the 15th day of the Hebrew month of Nisan (right after Passover).
- This Feast lasts for seven days.
- The first of these seven days and the last of the seven days are Sabbaths.
- Unleavened bread is required to be eaten during the entire 7-day period.
- This Feast is one of the three pilgrimage Feasts where all Israelite males were required to go to the Temple in Jerusalem to "appear before the Lord".
(Deuteronomy 16:16)

Details:

- The second of the Spring Feasts is named after the bread which is required to be eaten during this 7-day period. It is mentioned as a separate Feast on the 15th day of the same month as Passover but because it is clustered closely with Passover, the entire period is sometimes called Passover.

- Thus, Passover, Unleavened Bread, and First Fruits have all been incorporated into the celebration of Passover and reference to Passover usually means all three. Therefore, Passover is actually celebrated for eight days, Nisan 14-21.
- The "Feast of Unleavened Bread" is considered a Prominent Feast. Unlike the other Feasts which are listed and instituted after the Exodus during the wilderness sojourn in Leviticus 23, the commandment instituting this Feast was given prior to the Exodus from Egypt (Exodus 12:14-20).
- Passover and the Feast of Unleavened Bread were instituted first—while the details for the other Feasts came later.
- The Lord said that for seven days, the children of Israel must eat unleavened bread. This bread, made in a hurry without yeast, represents how the Lord brought His people out of Egypt in a haste.
- In scripture, leaven represents sin.
- Not only is eating bread with leaven during the Feast of Unleavened Bread unlawful, but even having leaven

present in your house or dwelling is forbidden because it represents the cleansing of sin from our lives.
- Thus, cleansing our house before Passover symbolizes our search to remove any known sin or hypocrisy in our lives.

Significant Facts about the Feasts of Unleavened Bread:
- The only type of bread eaten during the eight days of Passover and Feasts of Unleavened Bread is to be matzah.
- Matzah is bread made up with flour and water only, not any leaven (yeast). It is striped and pierced during baking to represent the Messiah.
- The utensils used must never touch leaven.
- Painstaking preparations are made weeks before the arrival of Passover and Unleavened Bread.
- Houses are cleaned, cooking utensils are scalded, clothing is washed with pockets turned inside out, carpets are cleaned, vacuum bags are discarded, and even special china dishes are brought out for the Feasts. Everything is scrubbed, scoured, cleaned, and aired in preparation for this Feast.

- Unleavened Bread in Scripture: Exodus 23:15-34, 34:18; 2 Chronicles 30; Ezra 6:22. In the 2nd Testament: Acts 12:3; 20:6.

The Mark of the Feasts!

"These are the LORD's appointed feasts...you are to proclaim at their appointed times... The LORD said to Moses, "Speak to the Israelites and say to them: 'When you enter the land I am going to give you and you reap its harvest, bring to the priest a sheaf of the first grain you harvest. He is to wave the sheaf before the LORD so it will be accepted on your behalf; the priest is to wave it on the day after the Sabbath... You must not eat any bread, or roasted or new grain, until the very day you bring this offering to your God. This is to be a lasting ordinance for the generations to come, wherever you live.'"
Leviticus 23:4, 9-14

Feasts of First Fruits
3rd of the Spring Feasts
Hebrew: Yom HaBikkurim (Yome Hah-Bee-koo-REEM)
(Also called - First Firstfruits)
Leviticus 23:9-14

General Facts:

- Observed in the early Spring (March/April).
- Occurs on the 16th day of the Hebrew month of Nisan — the 3rd in the festival cycle.
- Only two days after the beginning of the Passover season.
- First Fruits is the next-day Feast celebrated right after the Feast of Unleavened Bread.

Details:

- The series of the Spring Holy Days continues with the arrival of First Fruits, called Yom HaBikkurim or Sefirat Ha-Omer (*Hebrew for "the counting of the Omer*). First Fruits is named Sefirat Ha-Omer because of the "Counting the Omer".
- Since it comes on the heels of the major festival of Passover and Unleavened Bread, First Fruits is often overlooked.
- Scripture does not specify the actual calendar date of First Fruits (the waving of the sheaf offering), but merely

The Mark of the Feasts!

prescribes its time of observance to be "*on the day after the Sabbath*" (Leviticus 23:10-11).

- This leads to debates as to which Sabbath was in view — whether it referenced the actual 7th day Sabbath or the Feast of Unleavened Bread Sabbath. The majority opinion (held by the Pharisees) was that the Sabbath in question was Nisan 15, the first day of the Feast of Unleavened Bread. That day was to be a "holy convocation" on which no work was performed (Leviticus 23:7).

- Specifically, the chronology of the Passover season consists of: the first day of Passover, the second day of Feast of Unleavened Bread, and the third day of the Feast of First Fruits.

- The 2nd day of the Feasts of Unleavened (which is an 8-day celebration) is also called First Fruits. Thus, this 2nd day is a day simultaneously shared by both holidays (Unleavened Bread and First Fruits).

- On First Fruits, people offered the first ripe sheaf (first fruits) of barley to the Lord as an act of dedicating the harvest to Him. On Passover, a marked sheaf of grain was bundled and left standing in the field.

- On the next day, the first day of Unleavened Bread, the sheaf was cut and prepared for the offering on the third day.
- On this third day, Yom HaBikkurim, the priest waved the sheaves before the Lord in every direction—north, south, east, west, up, and down. By doing so, the whole crowd would be acknowledging God's provision and sovereignty over their lives and all the earth.
- Counting of the Days (Omer) then begins and continues until the day after the seventh Sabbath, the 50th day, which is called Shavuot or Pentecost (the next Feast on the calendar).
- Jewish people rarely celebrate Yom Habikkurim today, but it has great significance for followers of Yeshua as the most important day of the year, the day of His resurrection.

Biblical Events on this day:
- The manna which God provided from Heaven as food for the Israelites while they wandered in the wilderness, stopped after they crossed the Jordan River into the Promised Land (Joshua 5:10-12).
- Queen Esther risked her life to save the Jewish people (Esther 3:12-5:7).

The Mark of the Feasts!

- Yeshua rose from the dead on the third day. (Luke 24:44-47).
- Since the Temple was destroyed in 70 A.D., First Fruits sacrifices and offerings are no longer offered on this day. Today, this date begins the Counting of the Days (Omer). On the 33rd day of counting the Omer, a minor rabbinical holiday called Lag B-Omer is celebrated where campfires are built, people roast potatoes, and songs are sung.
- First Fruits is seen as a time-marker. It marks the beginning of the grain harvest in Israel, but more importantly, it marks the countdown of the Feast of Weeks, Shavuot, the fourth of the annual Feasts.
- Beginning with First Fruits, 49 (or seven sevens) are counted, and on the 50th day, the Feast of Weeks (called Pentecost or Shavuot) is celebrated.
- First Fruits is sometimes called "First First Fruits" because the next Feast in line, Feasts of Weeks (Shavuot) is called the "Day of Latter First Fruits".
- Feasts of First Fruits marks the beginning of the Spring barley harvest, while Shavuot (Feasts of Weeks) marks the beginning of the Summer wheat harvest.

"Chag Sah-meach Bikkurim!"
(Happy Festival of First Fruits!)

Angel Mariah

"These are the LORD's appointed feasts...you are to proclaim at their appointed times..." "From the day after the Sabbath, the day you brought the sheaf of the wave offering, count off seven full weeks. Count off fifty days up to the day after the seventh Sabbath, and then present an offering of new grain to the LORD... When you reap the harvest of your land, do not reap to the very edges of your field or gather the gleanings of your harvest. Leave them for the poor and for the foreigner residing among you."
Leviticus 23: 4, 15-22

The Mark of the Feasts!

Feasts of Weeks - Pentecost
4th of the Spring Feasts
1st of the late Spring Feasts
Hebrew: Shavuot (Sha-voo-OTE)
(Also called - Feast of Harvest & Latter First Fruits)
Leviticus 23:15-22

General Facts:

- Offerings are given and commemorates giving of the Law.
- The most common Hebrew designation was Hag Hashavuot, meaning "The Feasts of Weeks".
- Observed in the late Spring, usually May or early June.
- On the Hebrew calendar, the sixth day of the month of Sivan.
- One of the three triad of pilgrimage feasts when all males were required to go to Jerusalem to "appear before the Lord" (Deuteronomy 16:16).

Details:

- The day after Passover comes the Feasts of Unleavened Bread which lasts seven days (Nisan 15-21).
- Fifty days after Passover, Shavuot is celebrated. Also known as Pentecost, Feasts of Weeks, the Feasts of Harvest, and the Latter First Fruits, it is the time to

present an offering of new grain of the Summer wheat harvest to the Lord.

- The Feasts of Pentecost is counted 50 days from the first day (Nisan 15) of the Feast of Unleavened Bread.
- Shavuot is celebrated 50 days after Passover, so it became known as Pentecost, which means "50" in Greek.
- The word 'Pentecost' comes from the Greek word for the "50th day". "Pente" is Greek for five.
- It is called 'Shavuot' in Hebrew or the Feasts of Weeks (found in Exodus 34:22; Deuteronomy 16:9-11) and the Feasts of Harvest (Exodus 23:16) of the Day of the First Fruits (Numbers 28:26).
- The observance of the Feasts of Weeks or Pentecost is recorded in the Old Testament in Exodus 34:22, Leviticus 23:15-22, Deuteronomy 16:16, 2 Chronicles 8:13, and Ezekiel 1.
- Because it occurred at the conclusion of the Passover, it acquired the name "Latter First Fruits".

Details - Pentecost:
- It shows joy and thankfulness for the Lord's blessing of harvest. Often called 'Matin Torah' (giving of the Law), it is tied to the Ten Commandments because it is

The Mark of the Feasts!

believed God gave Moses the Ten Commandments at this time.

- The celebration of Shavuot was never tied to an actual calendar date in the Torah. It was, instead, defined as a calculation of 50 days (the day after seven weeks had passed) from the earlier Feast of First Fruits. *"And you shall count fifty days to the day after the seventh Sabbath"* (Leviticus 23:15-16 / Deuteronomy 16:9-10).
- Because of the commandment to count, the time period from First Fruits to Shavuot is known as Sefirah (Hebrew for 'counting').
- Historically, children receive treats for memorizing Scripture at Shavuot and the Book of Ruth is often read to celebrate the holiday.

Significant Facts:
- Shavuot is traditionally a joyous time of giving thanks and presenting offerings for the new grain of the Summer wheat harvest in Israel.
- Special foods are a tradition because the law is referred to milk and honey.
- Homes and synagogues are decorated with greenery, which represent the harvest and the Torah as a "Tree of Life".

- Observant Jews often spend the night reading and studying Torah.
- Feasts of Weeks in 1st Testament: Exodus 34:22; Deuteronomy 16:9; Ezekiel 1 (traditional reading).
- 2nd Testament Scripture: Acts 2:1-41; 20:16; 1 Corinthians 16:8; James 1:18.
- The name "Feasts of Weeks" was given because God commanded the Jews in Leviticus 23:15-16 to count seven full weeks (or 49 days) beginning on the second day of Passover, and then present offerings of new grain to the Lord as a lasting ordinance.
- Shavuot was originally a festival for expressing thankfulness to the Lord for the blessing of the harvest and because it occurred at the conclusion of the Passover, it acquired the name "Latter First Fruits".
- Pentecost or the Feasts of the First Fruits, falls on Sunday, the first day of the week "the morrow after the Sabbath" (see Leviticus 23:11, 23:15-16). It was 50 days after God delivered the children of Israel from captivity in Egypt when He gave them the Ten Commandments and the Law, establishing Israel as a nation.
- Because Shavuot is tied to the giving of the Ten Commandments — it thus bears the name Matin Torah or "Giving of the Law".

The Mark of the Feasts!

Other Significant Facts:

- Yeshua was resurrected on the first day of the week, on the day of First Fruits which was Sunday.
- The first "Fruit" was the Messiah, and the second "fruits" were those saved on the Day of Pentecost and those who have believed since.
- On this same day, 50 days after the crucifixion of Yeshua, God established the New Covenant Church in Jerusalem (as recorded in Acts 2).
- For the first time on the day of Pentecost, believers were permanently indwelled by the Holy Spirit and received the Baptism of the Holy Spirit, just as the Messiah promised on the day He ascended into Heaven (Acts 1:5-8).
- Empowered by the Holy Spirit, believers would spread out into Jerusalem and thence to Judea, Samaria, and out to the ends of the earth preaching the good news of the Kingdom. Some of the most exciting events in the New Testament revolve around the Day of Pentecost in the Book of Acts Chapter 2. Pentecost is also mentioned in Acts 20:16, 1 Corinthians 16:8, and James 1:18.
- Leviticus 23:17 records that two "wave" loaves of bread of equal weight were baked with leaven. These two loaves were called the "first fruits". The loaves represent

carnal man because leaven is used. They represent the Bride of Christ made up of Jews and Gentiles, both with sin, unlike the unleavened bread at Passover which represented a sinless Messiah.

Scripture References:
- *"And ye shall count unto you from the morrow after the Sabbath, from the day that ye brought the sheaf of the wave offering; seven Sabbaths shall be complete: Even unto the morrow after the seventh Sabbath shall ye number fifty days; and ye shall offer a new meat offering unto the LORD"* (Leviticus 23:15-16).
- *"And thou shalt observe the Feast of Weeks, of the first fruits of wheat harvest, and the Feast of Ingathering at the year's end"* (Exodus 34:22).
- *"Seven weeks shalt thou number unto thee: begin to number the seven weeks from such time as thou begin to put the sickle to the corn. And thou shalt keep the Feast of Weeks unto the LORD thy God with a tribute of a freewill offering of thine hand, which thou shalt give unto the LORD thy God, according as the LORD thy God hath blessed thee: And thou shalt rejoice before the LORD thy God, thou, and thy son, and thy daughter, and thy manservant, and thy maidservant, and the Levite that is within thy gates, and the stranger, and the fatherless, and the widow, that are among you, in the place*

The Mark of the Feasts!

which the LORD thy God hath chosen to place His name there" (Deuteronomy 16:9-11).

- "Also in the day of the first fruits, when ye bring a new meat offering unto the LORD, after your weeks be out, ye shall have an holy convocation; ye shall do no servile work" (Numbers 28:26).

The Interlude
The period between the Spring and Fall Feasts
(The Long, Hot Summer Months!)

With the close of Shavuot (Pentecost), we come to the end of the Spring season of the Holy Feasts Days.

It starts with the redemption of Passover (Pesach), followed by the resurrection of Feasts of Unleavened Bread (Hag HaMatzot) and Yom HaBikkurim (First Fruits) and culminates with the 50 days of the Counting of the Omer to the second of the First Fruits (Shavuot). Historically, these Spring Holy Days have already been fulfilled according to God's calendar of events.

Accordingly, there is now a gap of time during the long Summer in which there are no Biblical Holy Days. The crops will grow during the Summer months until the arrival of the Fall holidays that speak of events just prior to the second coming of Yeshua.

As Yeshua Himself said, "*Now learn a parable of the fig tree; when his branch is yet tender, and putteth forth leaves, ye know that Summer is nigh: So likewise, ye, when ye shall see all these things, know that it is near, even at the doors*" (Matthew 24:32-33).

The Mark of the Feasts!

We are presently in that long, hot Summer in which God is growing what will be harvested. Many signs indicate that the Summer is quickly drawing to a close and the fulfillment of the Fall Feasts Days are about to begin.

Like the farmer, now is the time to work to help bring in the harvest of the latter days. For sure, the Fall season will come.

"Behold, I come quickly:
blessed is he that keepeth the saying of the prophecy of this book."
(Revelation 22:7)

Overview of the Fall Feasts
(Comes in a cluster of three)

The final three Feasts Days (Holy Days, holidays) occur in the Fall of the year within a brief period in the Hebrew month of Tishri (September/October). As the first four Spring Feasts Days depict events associated with Yeshua's first coming, these final three Feasts Days depict specific events associated with His second coming. These final Feasts form the basis for what the Bible calls the ***"Blessed Hope!"*** (Titus 2:13).

The final three Fall Feasts are:

>1st = Trumpets
>
>Hebrew: Yom Teruah
>
>Blowing the Shofars and the New Year (Rosh Hashanah)
>
>
>2nd = Day of Atonement
>
>Hebrew: Yom Kippur
>
>Holiest Day of Year - Day of Fasting
>
>
>3rd = Tabernacles
>
>Hebrew: Sukkot
>
>Feasts of Booths, Shelters, Feasts of Ingathering
>
>One of the three triad of pilgrimage Feasts

The Mark of the Feasts!

ELUL

- Elul is the sixth month on the Hebrew calendar known as "the time of preparation" and begins the Fall Feasts with a 40-day counting season called Teshuvah.

TESHUVAH

- Teshuvah is the period of 40 days which begins on the first day of Elul—continuing on to the seventh month known as Tishri.
- The last 10 days of this 40-day season starts the month of Tishri and the Feasts of Trumpets (called Yom Teruah in Hebrew).
- These 10 days are called the "10 High Holy Days" and the "Days of Awe", which leads to the final day of Yom Kippur—the holiest day of the year!

TASHLICH

- Tashlich, meaning "casting off" in Hebrew, is a tradition that involves symbolically casting off the sins of the previous year by tossing pieces of bread or stones into a body of flowing water.
- Just as the water carries away the bits, so, too, are sins symbolically carried away with hopes to start the New Year with a clean slate.

Overview of Elul, Teshuvah, and Tashlich

The Month of Elul
(The 6th month on the Hebrew calendar)

- Elul is the sixth month on the Hebrew calendar known as "the time of preparation".
- The month of Elul begins a 40-day counting season called Teshuvah, which is the Hebrew word for "return" or "repentance".
- The following month after the sixth month of Elul is the seventh Hebrew month of Tishri.

The 40-Day Period of Teshuvah

- Teshuvah is a period of 40 days which begins on the first day of the sixth month known as Elul (30 days).
- Continuing on from these 30 days (the month of Elul), Teshuvah flows into the seventh month known as Tishri for 10 more days.
- The last 10-day period of Teshuvah ends the 40-day count on the tenth day of the month of Tishri.
- The last 10 days of this 40-day season starts the Feasts of Trumpets (called Yom Teruah in Hebrew) and are called the "10 High Holy Days" and the "Days of Awe".
- This 10-day period leads to the final day of Yom Kippur.

The Mark of the Feasts!

- Thus, the 40-day countdown ends on the tenth day of the month of Tishri, known in Hebrew as Yom Kippur or The Day of Atonement.
- This day is the holiest day of the year!

The Tradition of Tashlich - Overview

- Tashlich is a tradition that many Jews observe during the New Year called Rosh Hashanah.
- Tashlich means "casting off" in Hebrew and involves symbolically casting off the sins of the previous year by tossing pieces of bread or stones into a body of flowing water.
- Just as the water carries away the bits, sins are symbolically carried away in hopes to start the New Year with a clean slate.
- Tashlich was inspired by a verse uttered by the prophet Micah: *"God will take us back in love; God will cover up our iniquities; God will hurl all our sins into the depths of the sea"* (Micah 7:19).

The Month of Elul - Overview

Elul is the sixth month on the Hebrew calendar and is also known as "the time of preparation", just as the weekly 6-day Friday is known as "the day of preparation" for the seventh day Sabbath.

The following month, the seventh Hebrew month, is called Tishri on the Biblical calendar and as the seventh month, it parallels the seventh-day Sabbath as a special and holy time to rest and seek quiet time with God.

The first day of the month of Elul begins a 40-day season called Teshuvah, the Hebrew word for "return" or "repentance".

This period begins on the first day of Elul and ends 40 days later on the tenth day of the following month of Tishri.

The first 30 days of this 40-day season occur during the month of Elul (the sixth month) and the last 10 days of this 40-day season are the first 10 days of the month of Tishri.

This entire countdown of 40 days (the first of Elul through the tenth of Tishri) is the yearly time for one to examine

The Mark of the Feasts!

his life and restore relationships between himself and God, as well as with others.

The last 10 days of this 40-day season starts the Feast of Trumpets (called Yom Teruah in Hebrew) and are called the "10 High Holy Days" and the "Days of Awe".

These "10 High Holy Days" begin the new month of Tishri and mark the end of the 40-day countdown. Thus, the 40-day countdown ends on the tenth day of the month of Tishri, known in Hebrew as "Yom Kippur" or "The Day of Atonement".

"Yom Kippur" or "The Day of Atonement" is the holiest day of the year!

The 40-Day Period of Teshuvah
(Hebrew meaning: Return or Repentance)

- Teshuvah is the Hebrew word meaning "return" or "repentance".
- Preparation for the first of the Fall Feasts is called '40 Days of Teshuvah'.
- Teshuvah is a period of 40 days which begins on the first day of the sixth month known as Elul (30 days).
- On the Jewish civil calendar, this is a 40-day season.
- This period begins on the first day of the sixth month called Elul and ends on the tenth day of the following month of Tishri known as "The Day of Atonement" or "Yom Kippur", which is the holiest day of the year!
- This 40-day season is a time for one to yearly examine his life and restore relationships between himself and God, as well as others.
- The first 30 days of this season are the month of Elul (the sixth month).
- The last 10 days of this 40-day season are the Feasts of Trumpets and The Day of Atonement and the 10 High Holy Days called 'The Days of Awe'.

The Mark of the Feasts!

Why 40 Days?
'Significance of the Number 40'

- Genesis 6:3b says, *"...therefore their life span is to be 120 years"*. 120 is divisible by the number 40 three times.

- *"It rained on the earth forty days and forty nights"* (Genesis 7:12). What is the significance of the "40 days and 40 nights" of rain? The number 40 often represents a generation. God's rain judgment against that wicked generation lasted for "40 days and 40 nights".

- *"Moses entered the cloud and went up on the mountain; he was on the mountain forty days and forty nights"* (Exodus 24:18).

- *"Moses was there with GOD forty days and forty nights, during which time he neither ate food or drank water..."* (Exodus 34:28). What is the significance of Moses being on Mount Sinai for 40 days and 40 nights without food and water?

- Matthew 4:1-2 says, *"Then the Spirit led Yeshua up into the wilderness to be tempted by the Adversary. After Yeshua had fasted forty days and nights, He was hungry"*. Moses' 40 days and nights without food parallels the Messiah's 40 days and nights without food.

Another significant forty...

- Do you remember this story? Moses sent 12 spies into the Promised Land. They returned after 40 days and gave their report. Ten of the 12 spies gave a bad report and only Joshua and Caleb encouraged the people to go up to the land. The people refused to listen to Joshua and Caleb, rebelled against God, and did not enter the land. This was their punishment for sinning against God. *"Forty days later, they returned from exploring the land"* (Numbers 13:25).

- The 40 years Israel wandered in the wilderness correlates to the 40 days they explored the land and then refused to go into the land. *"But you, your carcasses will fall in this desert; and your children will wander about in the desert for forty years. It will be a year for every day you spent exploring the land that you will bear the consequences of your offenses, forty days, forty years"* (Numbers 14:32-34).

- How old was Joshua when he and the others explored the land? Joshua 14:7 says, *"I (Joshua) was forty years old when Moses the servant of GOD sent me from Kadesh Barnea to explore the land, and I brought back to him an honest report"*.

- Five times, Paul received the "forty lashes minus one" from the Jews (2 Corinthians 11:24).

The Mark of the Feasts!

- The 40 lashes were the **maximum** punishment a person could receive. The 40 lashes were reserved for the worst of offenders. Messiah received the maximum punishment.
- It is believed that Messiah received the "forty lashes minus one". "*Then, if the wicked one deserves to be flogged, the judge is to have him lie down and be flogged in his presence. The number of strokes is to be proportionate to his offense, but the maximum number is forty...*" (Deuteronomy 25:2-3)
- The Book of Judges also has sets of forty. "*So, the land had rest for forty years, until Othniel, son of Kenaz, died.*" (Judges 3:11)
- Israel had 40 years of peace when Deborah ruled. (Judges 5:31)
- "*During Gideon's lifetime, the land enjoyed peace for forty years.*" (Judges 8:28b)
- Judges 13:1 says, "*Again the Israelites did evil in the eyes of GOD, so that GOD delivered them into the hands of the Philistines for forty years*".
- The last leader of Israel (before King Saul) was the prophet Samuel. "*He (Samuel) led Israel for forty years.*" (1 Kings 2:11a)

- How long did King Solomon reign? *"Solomon reigned in Jerusalem over all Israel for forty years"* (1 Kings 11:42). Like father, like son. David was 30 years old when he began his reign (2 Samuel 5:4) and Messiah was also 30 years old when He started His ministry.
- Matthew 24:32-35 talks about a spiritual lesson from the fig tree. The fig tree represents Israel (see also Matthew 21:18-19). Messiah says that "this generation" will not pass away until all this happens (Matthew 24:3-31).
- Already mentioned, 40 years represents 'one generation'. When the fig tree (Israel) gets leaves and its twigs get tender, then there will be one generation (forty years) until Messiah returns. Some believers think we are living in that last generation. If that is the case, then what point in time did the fig tree (Israel) get leaves and tender twigs?
- Some people said that when Israel became a nation in 1948, that Messiah would return in 1988. There was even a book called *88 Reasons Why Christ is Coming Back in 1988*.
- There is an interesting parallel between the 40-year 'one generation' and the story of David and Goliath.

The Mark of the Feasts!

"For forty days, the Philistine (Goliath) came forward every morning and evening took his stand" (1 Samuel 17:16).

- Acts 1:3 states that Messiah remained on the earth for 40 days after His resurrection and then He ascended into Heaven (Acts 1:9). Messiah ascended after 40 days and He will again descend after 40 years (one generation).
- The Day of Atonement stands as a day of judgment and the 40 days prior (Elul 1 - Tishri 10) is a special time of repentance. It is believed that the flood waters of Noah began on the Day of Atonement (Tishri 10).
- We know that Moses lived to be 120 years old. Moses' life can be divided into three sets of four. Acts 7:22-23 says that Moses first set of 40 was when he was educated for 40 years in wisdom of the Egyptians. Moses' second set of 40 was when he was a wandering shepherd (Acts 7:30). This was Moses' preparation for his last set of 40 years.
- The third and last set of 40 was when Moses led Israel in the desert for 40 years and taught them God's Torah.

Examples of the Number 40 in the Bible

- The rains (in Noah's day) fell for 40 days and nights (Genesis 7:4).
- Isaac was 40 years old when he married Rebekkah (Genesis 25:20).
- Esau was 40 years old when he married Judith. (Genesis 26:34).
- Israel wandered in the desert and ate manna for 40 years (Exodus 16:35).
- Moses was with God on the mount for 40 days and nights (Exodus 24:18).
- The sockets of silver are in groups of 40 (Ex. 26:19, 21).
- Moses was again with God for 40 days and nights (Exodus 34:28).
- Moses was 40 years old when he first visited his people (Acts 7:23).
- Moses led Israel from Egypt at age 80 (2 times 40), and after 40 years in the wilderness, died at the age of 120 (3 times 40; Deuteronomy 34:7).
- Israel's spies explored the Promised Land of Canaan for 40 days (Numbers 13:25).

The Mark of the Feasts!

- Therefore, God made Israel wander for 40 years (Numbers 14:33-34).
- Forty stripes was the maximum penalty. (Deuteronomy 25:3)
- Caleb was 40 when he spied out the land of Canaan (Joshua 14:7).
- God allowed the land to rest for 40 years (Judges 3:11).
- God again allowed the land to rest for 40 years. (Judges 5:31).
- Jonah gave the city of Ninevah 40 days to repent or be destroyed.
- God again allowed the land to rest for 40 years. (Judges 8:28)
- Abdon (a judge in Israel) had 40 sons (Judges 12:14).
- Israel did evil; God gave them to the enemy for 40 years (Judges 13:1).
- Eli judged Israel for 40 years (1 Samuel 4:18).
- Goliath presented himself to Israel for 40 days. (1 Samuel 17:16)
- Saul reigned for 40 years (Acts 13:21).
- Ishbosheth (Saul's son) was 40 when he began his reign (2 Samuel 2:10).
- David reigned over Israel for 40 years. (2 Samuel 5:4; 1 Kings 2:11)

- The holy place of the Temple was 40 cubits long. (1 Kings 6:17)
- 40 baths (measurement) was size of lavers in the Temple (1 Kings 7:38).
- Solomon reigned same length as his father: 40 years. (1 Kings 11:42)
- Elijah had one meal that gave him strength for 40 days (1 Kings 19:8).
- Jehoash (Joash) reigned for 40 years in Jerusalem. (2 Kings 12:1)
- Egypt was laid desolate for 40 years (Ezekiel 29:11-12).
- Ezekiel's (symbolic) temple is 40 cubits long. (Ezekiel 41:2)
- Outer courts in Ezekiel's temple were 40 cubits long (Ezekiel 46:22).
- God gave Nineveh 40 days to repent (Jonah 3:4).
- Yeshua fasted 40 days and nights (Matthew 4:2).
- Yeshua was tempted for 40 days (Luke 4:2; Mark 1:13).
- Yeshua remained on earth 40 days after His resurrection (Acts 1:3).
- Finally, according to the Talmud (Judaism's holiest book), it takes 40 days for an embryo to be formed in its mother's womb.

The Tradition of Tashlich
(Hebrew meaning: Casting Off)

- Tashlich is a tradition that many Jews observe during Rosh Hashanah.

- Tashlich means "casting off" in Hebrew and involves symbolically casting off the sins of the previous year by tossing pieces of bread or stones into a body of flowing water. Just as the water carries away the bits, so, too, are sins symbolically carried away. In this way, the participant hopes to start the New Year with a clean slate.

- Tashlich was inspired by a verse uttered by the prophet Micah: *"God will take us back in love; God will cover up our iniquities; God will hurl all our sins into the depths of the sea"* (Micah 7:19).

- As the custom evolved, it became tradition to go to a river and symbolically cast your sins into the water on the first day of the New Year, Rosh Hashanah.

- Tashlich is traditionally performed on the first day of Rosh Hashanah but if this day falls on the Sabbath, then Tashlich isn't observed until the second day of Rosh Hashanah.

- If it is not performed on the first day of Rosh Hashanah, it can be done any time up until the last day of Sukkot, which is thought to be the last day of the New Year's "judgment" period.

- In order to perform Tashlich, take pieces of bread or stones and go to a flowing body of water such as a river, stream, sea, or ocean. Lakes or ponds that have fish are also good places, both because the animals will eat the food and because fish are immune to the evil eye.
- Some traditions say that fish are also significant because they can be trapped in nets—just as we can be trapped in sin.
- Recite the following blessing from Micah 7:18-20 and then toss the bits of bread into the water:

"Who is like You, God, who removes iniquity and overlooks
transgression of the remainder of His inheritance.
He does not remain angry forever because He desires kindness.
He will return and He will be merciful to us, and He will conquer
our iniquities and cast off our sins into the depths of the seas.
Give truth to Jacob, kindness to Abraham,
like that you swore to our ancestors from long ago."

- Tashlich has traditionally been a solemn ceremony but in recent years, it has become a very social mitzvah. People will often gather at the same body of water, then

The Mark of the Feasts!

they'll catch up with friends they haven't seen in a while afterward.

- In some communities, people will also pull out their pockets and shake them to make sure any lingering sins are cast off.

Angel Mariah

*"These are the LORD's appointed feasts... you are to proclaim
at their appointed times... "The LORD said to Moses,
Say to the Israelites: On the first day of the seventh month
you are to have a day of Sabbath rest, a sacred assembly
commemorated with trumpet blasts.
Do no regular work, but present
a food offering to the LORD."*
Leviticus 23: 4, 23-25

Feasts of Trumpets
(1st of the three Fall Feasts)
Hebrew: Yom Turuah
(Day of Sounding Shofar)
(Rosh Hashanah the New Year)
Leviticus 23:23-25

Specific Notes:

- This Feasts usually occurs in September.
- Unlike other Feasts, they do not celebrate a season or historical event. This is a time for looking inward to spiritual growth.
- The Feast of Trumpets is the only Feast on a new moon.
- Trumpets and The Day of Atonement are both the holiest days of the Jewish year.
- It is simply referred to as Yom Teruah (The Day of Sounding of the Shofar), so it became known as the Feasts of Trumpets.
- The Feasts of Trumpets calls attention to the coming of the holiest day of the year—Yom Kippur (The Day of Atonement)—which occurs 10 days later.
- The Feasts of Trumpets is also the Jewish New Year or Rosh Hashanah.

The Feasts of Trumpets falls on the first day of the Hebrew Civil Year in the month Tishri:

Tishri is the seventh month of the Biblical calendar and as such parallels the Sabbath as a special and holy time to seek God. The previous Hebrew month (sixth month) of Elul is the time of preparation, just as Friday is the Day of Preparation for Sabbath.

Leviticus 23 calls this Feast a "memorial":

Many believe it is a memorial of God's grace to Abraham when He substituted a ram to be sacrificed instead of Isaac (Genesis 22).

It is also regarded by both Jews and Gentiles as a memorial of the creation of the world at which the sons of God shouted for joy (Job 38:7).

The only Feast that falls on the first of the month:

It falls during the time of the dark (or first) sliver of the new moon.

All other Feasts fall in the middle of the month, during the time of the full moon when it is light. In this way, Israel celebrated the Feasts in the light. Without electricity, the light of the moon was most beneficial for travel to and from the Feasts.

The Mark of the Feasts!

This Feasts Day has no name.

It is simply referred to as Yom Teruah (The Day of Sounding of the Shofar), so it became known as the Feasts of Trumpets.

Ten Days of Awe:
- The Feasts of Trumpets calls attention to the coming of the holiest day of the year—The Day of Atonement (Yom Kippur)—which occurs 10 days later.
- Trumpets and The Day of Atonement are both the holiest days of the Jewish year.
- These 10 days between Trumpets and The Day of Atonement are called The Days of Awe or Days of Repentance, as well as the High Holy Days.

Preparation for the Feasts called Forty Days of Teshuvah:
- On the Jewish civil calendar is a 40-day season called Teshuvah, which is the Hebrew word meaning "return" or "repentance".
- This period begins on the first day of the sixth month called Elul and ends on the tenth day of the following month of Tishri known as "The Day of Atonement" or "Yom Kippur" which is the holiest day of the year!

- This 40-day season is a time for one to yearly examine his life and restore relationships between himself and God, as well as others.
- The first 30 days of this season are the month of Elul (the sixth month).
- The last 10 days of this 40-day season are the Feast of Trumpets and The Day of Atonement or the 10 High Holy Days called 'Days of Awe'.

Blowing the Shofar:

The priests chosen to blow the shofar were trained from childhood and the ceremony of the blowing of the shofar was a magnificent sight.

> *"Sound the Shofar in Zion and sound the alarm in my holy mountain: let all the inhabitants of the Land tremble: for the day of the LORD cometh, it is nigh at hand."*
> *Joel 2:1*

The Mark of the Feasts!

Jewish Customs of Trumpets

Trumpets require a preparing of the spirit:
- Each person is to take time to look back in self-examination over the events and emotions of the previous year.
- This is a time of offering forgiveness and seeking reconciliation with others (family, friends, and business associates).
- Make amends! Everyone is to seek out anyone who feels hurt or wronged and "clear the air" by asking for forgiveness and understanding for any harsh words said or deeds done during the past year.

The night before Rosh Hashanah:

A special midnight service is conducted called "Selichos" (Repentant Prayers) which helps to prepare for the time of reverence and self-appraisal during the coming Days of Awe.

Most Jews celebrate this holiday for two days:

Since the precise hour for the appearance of the new moon of Tishri could not always be ascertained, this Fesat was extended to two days. Reform Jews retain the practice of a one-day celebration.

The shofar is the highpoint of the service during Trumpets:
- The shofar-blower (Ba'al Tokea) prepares himself for his task of blowing the shofar for the congregation and says, "I am prepared to fulfill God's commandments to blow the shofar, as it is prescribed in the Torah; a day of blowing unto you".
- The end of the shofar is curved and bent as a reminder to bend in respect to God.
- The sound is meant to be a rousing call to repentance — to awaken everyone to make them remember the Creator, forsake evil ways, and return to God.
- The sound of the shofar is also meant to inspire as a reminder that all should strive to break the impulses of the carnal heart.

Four different sounds of the shofar associated with Trumpets:
- **Tekiah:**

    A pure, unbroken sound that calls man to search his heart and seek forgiveness through repentance.
- **Shevarim:**

    A broken, staccato, trembling sound. It typifies the sorrow that comes to man when he realizes his wrong and desires to change his ways.

The Mark of the Feasts!

- **Teruah:**

  A wave-like sound of alarm calling upon man to stand by the banner of God.

- **Tekiah Gedolah:**

  The prolonged, unbroken sound typifying a final invitation to sincere repentance and atonement.

The Dinner:

- Set a special table with your best tablecloth and dishes.
- Sweet cakes and sweet fruit are provided as symbols of the sweet year to come.
- The tradition of apples dipped in honey symbolize a "sweet new year".
- Reciting of the blessing, "Be it your will that a good and sweet year be renewed for us".

The Ceremony of Tashlich (casting the stones):

- A custom widely observed is the symbolic ceremony called "Tashlich".
- This is the casting of one's sins into a river, lake, or other body of water on the afternoon of the first day of the Feast of Trumpets (some use a stone or bread).
- This custom is supposedly derived from Micah 7:19 – *"He will turn again, He will have compassion upon us;*

He will subdue our iniquities; and Thou wilt cast all their sins into the depths of the sea".

Send New Year cards:

This is a good time to teach the children and make your own family cards!

Play games, make music, and dance:

This is a happy occasion and should be enjoyed!

Wishing each other a "Happy New Year!":

- Before leaving one another, during the services it is customary to bless one another with the blessing for the coming New Year: "May your name be inscribed in the Book of Life!"

"Shanah Tovah!" (in Hebrew).

The Mark of the Feasts!

The Civil and Religious Calendars

God set the sun, moon, planets, and stars in their courses as an elaborate time-keeping device that has not varied since the beginning of creation. By this, we understand His Feasts Days, the appointed times and seasons, which enables us to live in harmony with Him and His Creation.

The Western world uses the Gregorian calendar which is based on the sun, while the Hebrew calendar is split into 12 months based on the lunar moon cycle.

There are two calendars in the Bible: The **Civil Calendar** (Genesis 1:1 to Exodus 12) and the **Religious Calendar**. The first month in the civil calendar is Tishri starting in the Fall, about September. The seventh month is Nisan (Aviv) starting in the Spring, about the time of our March and April.

God changed the civil calendar to the religious calendar in Exodus 12:1. "...And the LORD spake unto Moses and Aaron in the land of Egypt, saying, This month shall be unto you the beginning of months; it shall be the first month of the year to you." Now Nisan is the first month of the religious calendar & Tishri the seventh month (Exodus 13:4).

Civil Calendar	Religious Calendar
1. Tishri	1. Nisan (Aviv)
2. Heshvan	2. Iyar
3. Kislev	3. Sivan
4. Tevet	4. Tammuz
5. Shevat	5. Av
6. Adar	6. Elul
7. Nisan	7. Tishri
8. Iyar	8. Heshvan
9. Sivan	9. Kislev
10. Tammuz	10. Tevet
11. Av	11. Shevat
12. Elul	12. Adar

The Mark of the Feasts!

Four Themes of Trumpets

New Year:
- Judaism has two calendars, similar to our culture's New Year's Day (starting in January) and the business fiscal year (starting in July and ending in September). There is a Civil calendar and a Religious calendar.
- Religious calendar—The New Year starts in the Spring month of Nisan which contains Passover.
- Civil calendar—The New Year is the first day of the seventh month of Tishri called Rosh Hashanah.

God's Royalty (Coronation):
- It is said that on this day God manifests His royalty, the day He created His world, is also the day He sits in judgment.
- *"With trumpets and sound of cornet make a joyful noise before GOD, the King"* (Psalms 98:6).
- *"Lift up your heads, O ye gates; and be ye lift up, ye everlasting doors; and the King of glory shall come in. Who is this King of glory? GOD strong and mighty, GOD mighty in battle. Lift up your heads, O ye gates; even lift them up, ye everlasting doors; and the King of glory shall come in. Who is this King of glory? GOD of hosts, He is the King of glory"* (Psalms 24:7-10).

Day of Judgment:

The sages say that on this day, God has three scrolls that are opened:

1. Book of Righteousness — inscribed in the Book of Life.
2. Book of Wicked — recorded in the Book of Death.
3. Intermediates — not yet judged and have 10 more days to repent. If they repent before The Day of Atonement, their names will be written in the Book of Righteousness.

Remembrance:

The theme of "remembered" is thought to be from God, remembering Sarah and Hannah:

"Then they that feared the LORD spake often one to another: and the LORD hearkened, and heard it, and a book of remembrance was written before him for them that feared the LORD, and that thought upon His name. And they shall be mine, saith the LORD of hosts, in that day when I make up my jewels; and I will spare them, as a man spareth his own son that serveth him. Then shall ye return, and discern between the righteous and the wicked, between him that serveth God and him that serveth Him not" (Malachi 3:16-18).

Birthday of the world:

Jewish tradition believes this day is the birthday of the world because the first part of Genesis, Bereishit ("in the beginning"), when changed around, read Aleph b'Tishir (or "on the first of Tishri"). Therefore, the Feasts of Trumpets is known as the "Birthday of the World".

Messianic Significance of Trumpets

Sign of the return of Christ and a Memorial of grace to Abraham:

- Isaac, Abraham's son, is a type of foreshadowing of the Messiah.
- Just as Abraham offered his son, Isaac, on the altar, God offered His Son on Calvary's altar.
- *"By faith Abraham, when he was tried, offered up Isaac: and he that had received the promises offered up his only begotten son, of whom it was said, that in Isaac shall thy seed be called: accounting that God was able to raise him up, even from the dead; from whence also He received in Him a figure"* (Hebrews 11:17-19).
- Both Isaac's and Messiah's births were miracles.
- Both were obedient to the point of sacrifice.
- Both carried their own wood.

Trumpets point to the believer's victory in spiritual warfare:

"And having spoiled principalities and powers, he made a shew of them openly, triumphing over them in it" (Colossians 2:15).

Trumpets used in signals of war:

    Yeshua is the Commander of the Army of God.

Trumpets point to the believer's need to have a repentant heart:

- Our sins are not forgiven just because we believe.
- James 2:19 says, "*Thou believest that there is one God; thou doest well; the devils also believe and tremble*".
- To be forgiven, we must have a repentant heart. We must come in submission, asking for forgiveness, knowing that He will forgive us. That forgiveness has been guaranteed, bought, and paid for by the Messiah's atoning sacrifice on a tree.

The Messiah birth:

- Evidence shows that Yeshua was born in the Fall.
- It is believed that His baptism was also in the Fall.
- After His baptism, He spent 40 days in the wilderness (Matthew 4:1-2).
- It is possible these 40 days parallel the 40-day season called Teshuvah.
- Some believe this is the time He began His ministry — at the end of the 40 days.

    "*From that time on, He preached,*
"*Repent, for the kingdom of Heaven is at hand*" (Matthew 4:17).

The Mark of the Feasts!

Prophetic Significance of Trumpets

Feast of Trumpets is a major festival:

The three major festivals are Passover, Pentecost, and Feast of Trumpets.

Trumpets was the signal for the field workers to come into the Temple:

- The high priest blew the trumpet so it could be heard in the fields.
- The workers would stop harvesting, even if there were more crops, and leave immediately for worship service.

The 100 Trumpet Blasts:

- …announced the setting up of the eternal court with trumpets heralding God as the All-Seeing, All-Knowing Judge of the Universe.
- …court date to find out who is righteous and have their names written in the Book of Life.
- …all other people were a mixture of good and bad. God, in His mercy, will delay their court day for a period of time to allow them to prepare.
- The next court date is on Yom Kippur — The Day of Atonement.

- According to Jewish eschatology, the Pearly Gates of Heaven are opened on Trumpets (Rosh Hashanah) and closed on Yom Kippur.

The Second Coming of the Messiah:

It is possible that Trumpets will be fulfilled when the Messiah returns:

"For GOD Himself shall descend from Heaven with a shout, with the voice of the archangel, and with the trump of God: and the dead in Christ shall rise first: then we which are alive and remain shall be caught up together with them in the clouds, to meet GOD in the air: and so, shall we ever be with GOD" (1 Thessalonians 4:16-17).

According to Jewish tradition, the following happened on Tishri 1:

- The Feast of Trumpets is the only Feast on a new moon.
- Adam and Eve were created.
- The flood waters dried up.
- Enoch was taken to Heaven by God (Genesis 5:24).
- Joseph was freed from prison by Pharaoh.
- Forced labor of the Hebrews in Egypt ended.
- Job contracted leprosy.
- Start of the sacrifices on the altar built by Ezra (Ezra 3:1).

The Mark of the Feasts!

Sounding the Shofar

The 40 days of Teshuvah:

- 30 Days of Repentance
- 10 Days of Awe
- Day of Atonement — Yom Kippur (most holy day of the year)

The shofar is sounded every day for the 40 days in the morning to call all Israel to repentance. Each morning it is blown (single shavarim) in the four directions of the compass (East, North, West, South) to call each of the three tribes according to their position around the Wilderness Sanctuary. Traditionally, Judah is called first (East) because Judah means "praise" and Judah (praise to GOD) was always sent first into battle. The position of the 12 tribes is as follows:

- **East** — Judah, Issachar, Zebulun
- **North** — Dan, Naphtali, Asher
- **West** — Ephraim, Manasseh, Benjamin
- **South** — Reuben, Gad, Simeon

Sounding of the Shofar:

Takiah — one long, straight sound.
Teruah — nine or more short, staccato blasts (sounds like crying out — our plea for mercy).

Shevarim — broken; three low to high, medium length notes (sounds of our being broken).

Tekiah Gadola — one long blast announcing the final Divine Decree; held as long as possible; symbolizes His holding on to us; the "last great blast" (Exodus 19:13).

The Last Great Trump - Day of Atonement:

- Last Great Tekiah Gadola of the Trump of God — one long blast at His return, announcing the final moment of Eternal Atonement; it is finished!
- *"For GOD Himself shall descend from Heaven with a shout…with the trump of God: and the dead in Christ shall rise first."* (1 Thessalonians 4:16)
- *"…at the last trump: for the trumpet shall sound, and the dead shall be raised incorruptible, and we shall be changed."*
 (1 Corinthians 15:52)

The Mark of the Feasts!

A Valley of Dry Bones

"I was carried away by the Spirit of the Lord to a valley filled with bones...They were scattered everywhere across the ground and were completely dried out. Then He asked me, "Son of man, can these bones become living people again?" "O Sovereign Lord," I replied, "You alone know the answer to that." Then He said to me, "Speak a prophetic message to these bones and say, 'Dry bones, listen to the word of the Lord! This is what the Sovereign Lord says:
Look! I am going to put breath into you and make you live again! I will put flesh and muscles on you and cover you with skin. I will put breath into you, and you will come to life. Then you will know that I am the Lord.'" So, I spoke this message, just as He told me.

Angel Mariah

Suddenly as I spoke, there was a rattling noise all across the valley. The bones of each body came together and attached themselves as complete skeletons. Then as I watched, muscles and flesh formed over the bones. Then skin formed to cover their bodies, but they still had no breath in them. Then He said to me, "Speak a prophetic message to the winds...and say, 'This is what the Sovereign Lord says: Come, O breath, from the four winds! Breathe into these dead bodies so they may live again.'" So, I spoke the message as He commanded me, and breath came into their bodies. They all came to life and stood up on their feet - a great army! Then He said to me, "Son of man, these bones represent the people of Israel. They are saying, 'We have become old, dry bones - all hope is gone. Our nation is finished.' Therefore, prophesy to them and say, 'This is what the Sovereign Lord says: O my people, I will open your graves of exile and cause you to rise again. Then I will bring you back to the land of Israel. When this happens, O my people, you will know that I am the Lord. I will put my Spirit in you, and you will live again and return home to your own land. Then you will know that I, the Lord, have spoken, and I have done what I said. Yes, the Lord has spoken!"

Ezekiel 37:1-14 (NLT)

The Mark of the Feasts!

"These are the LORD's appointed feasts... you are to proclaim at their appointed times..." The LORD said to Moses, "The tenth day of this seventh month is the Day of Atonement. Hold a sacred assembly and deny yourselves, and present a food offering to the LORD. Do not do any work on that day, because it is the Day of Atonement, when atonement is made for you before the LORD your God... It is a day of Sabbath rest and you must deny yourselves. From the evening of the ninth day of the month until the following evening you are to observe your Sabbath."
Leviticus 23:4, 26-32

Feasts Day of Atonement
Second of the Three Fall Feasts
(Hebrew: Yom Kippur)
"Holiest Day of the Year"
Leviticus 23:26-32

The holiest day of the year is an ever-present theme woven through the entire pages of the Torah. Three and a half millennia after its divine institution, this holy day still wields a powerful influence over the entire culture and worship of Israel.

Holiest Day of the Year:

- This Holy Day occurs in the autumn, roughly corresponding to September or October.
- This Feasts falls on the tenth day of the month of Tishri, the seventh Hebrew month.
- This Feast falls 40 days following the Teshuvah count of the 40 days, which begins on the sixth month of Elul and runs through the first 10 days in the seventh month of Tishri.
- This Holy Day is observed between two other major Biblical holidays: Trumpets and Feasts of Tabernacles or Sukkot.

The Mark of the Feasts!

- Three separate Biblical passages outline this observance: Leviticus 16 for the high priest; Leviticus 23:26-32 for the people; and Numbers 29:7-11 for the sacrifices.

Day of Atonement

- Yom Kippur is the final day of judgment when God judges the world.
- The Hebrew word for Day of Atonement is Yom Kippur.
- "Yom" means 'day' and "Kippur" means 'atonement' or 'covering'.
- It is the most solemn holy day of the Hebrew year and is often referred to as "The Day".
- It is also The Day of Reconciliation between God and man.
- The time between Rosh Hashanah (the New Year) and Yom Kippur are called the "Ten Days of Awe" or the "Days of Repentance".
- This 10-day period is devoted to the spiritual exercises of repentance, prayer, and fasting.
- The number "10" symbolizes perfect holiness as the aim for all believers.
- It is designated by God as a day in which "*you shall afflict your souls*" (Leviticus 23:27,32).

- By definition, this term is understood to mean "fasting" (Ezra 8:21).
- **This is the only fast mandated by in the Torah.** It is to be observed by all males over the age of 13 and all females over the age of 12.
- The Israelite who failed to devote himself to fasting and repentance on Yom Kippur was to be "*cut off from his people*" (Leviticus 3:29).
- No work is done on this day, including at home. Many Jews spend the day at synagogues praying for the forgiveness of their sins. Immediately after the evening service, they have a "break-fast" meal.
- Services are held on this day from early morning until night. At sunset, the day is ended by a single blast of the shofar.
- The shofar (a ram's horn) is blown at the end of the evening prayer service for the first time since Rosh Hashanah.
- The Book of Jonah is read during the afternoon service to remind people of God's forgiveness and mercy.

The Ark of the Covenant:

- The Ark of the Covenant was seen only on this national day of repentance.

The Mark of the Feasts!

- When Solomon's temple was destroyed by the Babylonians (586 B.C.), the Ark was lost—never mentioned again in Scripture and never restored to Herod's second temple.
- Many speculate the Ark was hidden.

In the Home for Believers:

- With Erev Yom Kippur (the evening of Yom Kippur) approaching late in the afternoon on the ninth of Tishri, special arrangements are made to usher in the holiest day of the year.
- Since it is called a Sabbath, the general customs for the Sabbath are in order.
- The later afternoon holiday meal becomes more vital.
- The table is set with the best white linen and silver.
- It is customary to wear white on this Holy Day.
- Many families bless their children (parents, spouses) after the meal, saying a prayer over each child praying specifically for their needs, gifts, and talents.
- Throughout the High Holy Days, white holds a special meaning as it symbolizes our hope for purity and forgiveness. A sumptuous dinner is then served, which may include sweet dishes to represent the sweet new year of forgiveness.

- The fast traditionally includes abstaining from both food and drink (including water), abstaining from marital relations, using cosmetics and lotions, and washing any part of the body other than the fingers and eyes.
- A special memorial white candle is kindled to burn throughout the day.
- Since the Jews worldwide are packed into synagogues on this day, prayers for light to come and the reality of Yeshua the Messiah to enter their hearts are spoken. It is a special time to *"pray for the peace of JerUSAlem."* (Psalms 122:6)

Fascinating Facts:
- After destruction of the Temple in 70 A.D., people could no longer offer the prescribed sacrifices for atonement from sins. Today, they have substituted prayer, good works, and charitable donations hoping to take away the penalty for their sins.
- The modern observance of Yom Kippur bears very little resemblance to its Biblical observance. Today, it is based more upon the traditions of men than upon the pattern established in God's Law. This is mainly established upon acts of lovingkindness.

The Mark of the Feasts!

Messianic Significance:
- When Yeshua died on the cross, the thick veil ripped from top to bottom (Luke 23:44-46).
- Christ came as High Priest and entered the Holy of Holies (Heaven itself) once and for all — not by the blood of goats and calves, but by His own blood, having obtained eternal redemption (Hebrews 9:11-28).
- Believers in Yeshua accept His sacrifice on the cross as the final atonement for sin.
- When Messiah returns, Israel will look on Him who they pierced and repent (Zechariah 12:10).
- On this day of repentance, Israel will be forgiven and permanently restored (Isaiah 66:7-14; Romans 11:26).

Facts About the High Priest on Yom Kippur:
- Yom Kippur provides a good understanding of the scope of the Messiah's sacrifice and the security of God's people today.
- Three separate passages outline the Biblical observance.
- Divine priestly instructions given to the high priest (Leviticus 16).

- Yom Kippur is a very solemn day for the priesthood of Israel. Only on that singular day of the year was the high priest permitted to enter the Holy of Holies in the Temple and stand before the presence of God's powerfully electric Shekinah Glory.
- The high priest was required to wear holy garments woven from white linen, instead of his normal colorful garments overlaid with the golden breastplate.
- On Yom Kippur, the high priest changed clothing five times, and five times he followed the same cleansing procedure.
- His linen garments were worn only on this day and never again.
- High priests were required to leave home one week before and stay inside the Temple.
- The afternoon Temple service was the main focus of the Yom Kippur observance.
- Through the sacrifice of this service, atonement was made for the sins of the priest and the people of Israel for the preceding year.

The Mark of the Feasts!

The Red Thread:

- Tradition states that "a cord of red wool thread" was tied on the horn of a scapegoat before it was let go in the wilderness.
- A red thread of wool was also tied to the door of the sanctuary and when the scapegoat reached the wilderness, the thread turned white.
- When the red thread turned white, it was a sign that God forgave the people's sins, for it is written in Isaiah 1:18, "*Though your sins be as scarlet, they shall be as white as snow*".
- Jewish literature states, "God's Shekinah Glory left the Temple 40 years prior to destruction".
- The Rabbis teach that during the last 40 years prior to the destruction of the Temple, the red thread no longer turned white supernaturally, nor did the western-most light shine, and the doors of the hekel (main sanctuary doors) would open by themselves.
- Spiritually, this indicated that God was no longer forgiving the sins of the people.

Angel Mariah

JerUSAlem
"The Center of the World"

JerUSAlem is not to be compared with any place else on earth. JerUSAlem is uniquely different. It stands absolutely alone among all the cities of the earth. Everyone on the earth is affected, in one way or another, by the city of JerUSAlem. In the Torah, according to Ezekiel 5:5, JerUSAlem is the *"Center of the Earth"*:

"Our feet shall stand within thy gates, O Jerusalem. Jerusalem is builded as a city that is compact together: ...Pray for the peace of Jerusalem: they shall prosper that love thee.
Peace be within thy walls, and prosperity within thy palaces"
(Psalm 122:2-3, 6-7).

"Thus saith the Lord God; This is Jerusalem:
I have set it in the midst of the nations and countries
that are round about her"
(Ezekiel 5:5).

"As the navel is set in the center of the human body,
so is the land of Israel the navel of the world...
situated in the center of the world,
and Jerusalem in the center of the land of Israel,
and the sanctuary in the center of Jerusalem,
and the holy place in the center of the sanctuary,
and the ark in the center of the holy place,
and the foundation stone before the holy place,
because from it the world was founded."

Midrash Tanchuma, Qedoshim.

The Mark of the Feasts!

YOM KIPPUR
The Day of Atonement
(The Holy of Holies!)

God's world is great and holy.
The holiest land in the world is the land of Israel.
In the land of Israel, **the holiest city** is Jerusalem.
In Jerusalem, **the holiest place** *was the Temple*,
and in the Temple was **the holiest spot**,
the Holy of Holies...
There are seventy peoples in the world.
The **holiest** among these is the people of Is-ra-el.
The holiest of the people of Israel is the tribe of Levi.
In the tribe of Levi, the **holiest are the priests**.
Among the priest, the **holiest was the High Priest**.
There are 354 days in the (lunar) year.
The holiest of these days are the **holy Feast days**.
Holier than these is the **Holy Sabbath Days**.
Among Sabbaths, the **holiest** is
The Day of Atonement, the Sabbath of Sabbaths...
There are 70 languages in the world;
the holiest is the Hebrew language.
Holier than all words in this language is **the Holy Torah;**
in the Torah the **holiest part is the Ten Commandments.**
In the Ten Commandments, the holiest of all the words
is the name of **God-Yhvh!**
And once during the year, at a certain hour,
these supreme **Holy of Holies of the world** *come together
and join as* **ONE!**

Angel Mariah

*"These are the LORD's appointed feasts... you are to proclaim at
their appointed times..." "So beginning with the fifteenth day
of the seventh month, after you have gathered the crops of the land,
celebrate the festival to the LORD for seven days;
the first day is a day of Sabbath rest, and the eighth day also is
a day of Sabbath rest... This is to be a lasting ordinance for the
generations to come; celebrate it in the seventh month.
Live in temporary shelters for seven days: All native-born Israelites
are to live in such shelters so your descendants will know
that I had the Israelites live in temporary shelters
when I brought them out of Egypt."
Leviticus 23:4, 39-43*

The Mark of the Feasts!

Feasts of Tabernacles
Third of the Fall Feasts
Hebrew: Sukkot
(Feast of Booths, Ingathering)
Leviticus 23:33-43 / Numbers 29:12-39
Deuteronomy 31:10-13 / Exodus 23:16, 34:22

Specific Notes:

- The seventh and final Feast in the seventh Hebrew month of Tishri.
- Sukkot is celebrated on the light of the full moon of the month of Tishri.
- The most prominent Feast, mentioned more often in Scripture than any others.
- The most joyful and festive of all of the seven Feasts.
- Known by two names: Sukkot and Tabernacles.
- Known also in Torah as "Feasts of Lights", commemorating the pillar of fire that led the children of Israel by night in the wilderness.
- Also known in Scripture as "The Feasts of Ingathering" (Exodus 23:16; 34:22) because it was observed after all crops had been gathered and harvested.
- Referred by the ancient Rabbis as simply "The Holiday".
- The first day of Tabernacles and the day after the seven-day period, the eighth day (known as Shemini Atzeret),

are considered sacred assemblies or Sabbaths (Leviticus 23:36,39).
- No work of any kind is permitted on these two days.
- The seventh and final day of Tabernacles is known as Hoshana Rabbah or "Great Hosanna".
- This Feast celebrated with great joy for two reasons:
  1. Commemorates God's past goodness and provision during the wilderness sojourn; and
  2. Commemorates God's present goodness and provision with the harvest.
- A Sukkah (Hebrew: Sukkot, often translated as "booth") is a temporary hut constructed during the week-long Feast of Sukkot.
- It is topped with branches and often well-decorated with autumn, harvest, or sacred items and/or themes.

Who:

- One of the three triad of pilgrimage Feasts when all males were required to go to JerUSAlem to "appear before the Lord" (Deuteronomy 16:16).
- It was a joyous pilgrimage with much singing and laughing along the way.
- The Torah requires all Israelites to dwell in tabernacles or temporary shelters during this Feast (Lev. 23:42-43).

The Mark of the Feasts!

- Great number of required sacrifices during Feast week — each day, one goat, 14 lambs, two rams, and two bullocks (13 on day one, decreasing by one each day).
- Each sacrifice offered with appropriate meal offerings (flour and oil) and drink offerings (wine).
- All 24 divisions of priests shared in the sacrificial duties during the week.
- **Solomon dedicated the newly-built Temple to the Lord during the Feasts of Tabernacles and the Shekinah Glory of the Lord descended from Heaven to light the fire on the altar.**

When:
- Seventh and final of the Fall Feasts.
- Occurs on the fifteenth day of Tishri — the seventh Hebrew month.
- Occurs in the autumn of the year (usually late September to mid-October).
- Observed five days after the solemn Day of Atonement.
- Lasts for seven days.
- At sundown, blast of the shofar (ram's horn) from the Temple announced the arrival.
- Observed after all crops have been harvested and gathered.

- Marks the beginning of the winter rainy season; thus, anticipation of rain is at its highest.
- The *prayer for rain* was an important part of observance.
- Celebration of water-pouring (not the ceremony itself) was observed during the evening of the Feasts by an impressive light ceremony known as the 'Simcha Bet Hasho'ayva' ("The Rejoicing of the House of Water-Drawing").
- Four towering menorahs (lampstands), each with four branches of oil lamps, were lit in the center of the court which flooded the Temple and the streets of JerUSAlem with light.
- The Levites sang the 15 Psalms of Degrees (Psalms 120-134) as they descended with each step down the 15 steps leading to the Court of Women.
- This celebration was repeated every night from the second night to the final night.
- This light celebration was reminiscent of the Shekinah glory during the dedication of Solomon's Temple and looked forward to the return of the Shekinah in the days of the coming Messiah (Ezekiel 43:1-6).
- Levites sang the hallel (the praise Psalms 113-118).
- On the seventh and final day of the Feast, the Temple reached a climax.

The Mark of the Feasts!

- Tradition held that it was on this day that God declared whether there would be rain for the coming year's crops.
- On the other six days, the silver trumpets gave three blasts.
- On this day, the seventh day, the trumpets gave three sets of seven blasts.
- On the other six days, the priest made one circuit around the altar.
- On this day, the priest made seven circuits while singing Psalm 118:25. The people waved palm branches.
- For this reason, the seventh and final day was known as Hoshana Rabbah or "Great Hosanna".

Where:
- One of the three pilgrim Feasts where pilgrimage to JerUSAlem was required.

Why:
- Celebrated with great joy for two reasons:
  1. Commemorates God's past goodness and provision during the 40-year wilderness sojourn; and
  2. Commemorates God's present goodness and provision with the harvest.

- Marks the beginning of the winter rainy season; thus, anticipation of rain is at its highest.
- The *prayer for rain* was an important part of observance.

Messianic Significance:
- Jewish literature states that the Shekinah glory left the Temple 40 years prior to its destruction in 70 A.D.
- The Rabbis teach that during the last 40 years prior to the destruction of the Temple, the red thread no longer turned white supernaturally, nor did the western-most light shine, and the doors of the hekel (main sanctuary doors) would open by themselves.
- The Messiah died approximately 40 years before the second Temple was destroyed, proving the timeline for His death (described as an "atoning death"). He rose from the dead showing that His atonement was accepted by the Father in Heaven.
- After the destruction of the Temple in 70 A.D., the Temple was no longer the place where atonement was accomplished.
- People could no longer offer the prescribed sacrifices for atonement from sins.
- It was, instead, in the permanent, once-for-all sacrifice of the Messiah.

The Mark of the Feasts!

- Yeshua came as High Priest and entered the Holy of Holies (Heaven itself) once and for all, not by the blood of goats and calves but by His own blood, having obtained eternal redemption (Hebrews 9:11-28).
- Believers in Yeshua accept His sacrifice on the cross as the final atonement for sin.
- When Yeshua died on the cross, the thick veil was ripped from top to bottom (Luke 23:44-46).
- When Yeshua returns, Israel will look on Him who they pierced and repent (Zechariah 12:10). On this day of repentance, Israel will be forgiven and permanently restored (Isaiah 66:7-14; Romans 11:26).
- Today, the Jewish people have substituted prayer, good works, and charitable donations to take away the penalty for their sins.
- They hold services on this day from early morning until night.
- The modern observance of Yom Kippur holds very little resemblance to its Biblical observance. Today, it is based more upon the traditions of men than upon the pattern established in God's Law. This is mainly established upon acts of lovingkindness.

How to Build a Sukkah
(The basics of building a sukkah and living inside it)

General Information:

- For 40 years, the children of Israel wandered in the Sinai desert prior to their entry into the Holy Land where miraculous "clouds of glory" surrounded and hovered over them, shielding them from the dangers and discomforts of the desert.
- Since that time, the tradition of building a sukkah (Hebrew for 'booths') has been observed to remember God's kindness and reaffirm trust in His providence by "dwelling" in a sukkah for the duration of the Sukkot Festival, from the fifteenth through the twenty-second of the Hebrew month of Tishri.
- This tradition is taken from Leviticus 23:42-43 – *"For a seven-day period, you shall live in booths"*.
- A sukkah is essentially an outdoor hut that is covered with vegetation, known as sechach.
- In Israel, there are many guidelines and requirements that must be followed in the construction of the sukkah and regarding the location where it is erected in order for a sukkah to be deemed "kosher" and fit for use.

Where to Build a Sukkah:

- Construct your sukkah outdoors, ideally in a spot that's most accessible to your residence. Popular sukkah locations include: porches, backyards, courtyards, lawns, balconies, and rooftops—basically, any location under the open sky.
- An important requirement is that there should be nothing between your sukkah and the open sky, so make sure that there are no trees, canopies, or roofs of any sort overhanging.
- A sukkah must be built anew every year.
- There are prefabricated sukkahs available in a variety of sizes from many Judaica vendors.

What Materials You Need:

- *The Walls:* The walls of a sukkah can be made of any material, provided they are sturdy enough that they do not move in a normal wind. You can use wood or fiberglass panels, waterproof fabrics attached to a metal frame, etc. You can also use pre-existing walls (i.e. the exterior walls of your home, patio, or garage) as one or more of the sukkah walls. An existing structure that is roofless or has a removable roof can also be made into a sukkah by covering it with proper sechach.

- *The Roof Covering:* The sukkah needs to be covered with sechach—raw, unfinished vegetable matter. Common sukkah roof-coverings are: bamboo poles, evergreen and palm branches, reeds, corn stalks, narrow strips (1x1 or 1x2) of unfinished lumber, or special sechach mats.
- *Mats:* Mats made of bamboo, straw, or other vegetable matter can be used only if they were made for the purpose of serving as a roof covering.
- *Lighting:* If you'd like to set up a lighting system and your sukkah is built close to an outlet, purchase a lightbulb with a rain protection cover and electrical cord.
- *Chairs and Tables:* Remember, you will be taking all your meals in the sukkah for the duration of the festival. Plus, it is a special commandment (mitzvah) to invite guests to share your sukkah.
- *Decorations:* Many people decorate the sukkah with colorful posters depicting holiday themes, by hanging memorabilia and fresh fruits or other decorations from the sechach beams or both.

The Walls:

- A sukkah must have at least two full walls plus part of a third wall (the "part" needs to be a minimum of

The Mark of the Feasts!

3.2 inches wide). It is preferable, however, that the sukkah have four complete walls.

The Sechach:

- There must be sufficient sechach (vegetation) to provide enough shade so that in a bright midday, there is more shade than sun seen on the floor of the sukkah.

Sukkot - Messiah's Birth

Was the Messiah conceived on Hanukkah and born during the time of Sukkot:

- Many believe that the Messiah, the "Light of the World", was conceived on the Festival of Lights (Hanukkah). The Torah does not specifically say the date of Yeshua's birth but we know, however, that it was not during the Winter months because the sheep were in the pasture (Luke 2:8).
- A study of the time of the conception of John the Baptist reveals that John was conceived around Sivan 30 (the eleventh week) (Luke 1:8-15, 24).

"And it came to pass, that while he executed the priest's office before God in the order of his course, according to the custom of the priest's office, his lot was to burn incense when he went into the temple of the Lord. And the whole multitude of the people were praying without at the time of incense. And there appeared unto him an angel of the Lord standing on the right side of the altar of incense. And when Zacharias saw him, he was troubled, and fear fell upon him. But the angel said unto him, Fear not, Zacharias: for thy prayer is heard; and thy wife Elisabeth shall bear thee a son, and thou shalt call his name John. And thou shalt have joy and gladness; and many shall rejoice at his birth. For he shall be great in the sight of the Lord, and shall drink neither wine nor strong drink;

The Mark of the Feasts!

and he shall be filled with the Holy Ghost, even from his mother's womb. And after those days his wife Elisabeth conceived, and hid herself five months..."

- Adding 40 weeks for a normal pregnancy, it reveals that John the Baptist was born on or about Passover (Nisan 14). Six months after John's conception, Mary conceived Yeshua (Luke 1:26-33).

" And in the sixth month the angel **Gabriel** *(a very special angel) was sent from God unto a city of Galilee, named Nazareth, to a virgin espoused to a man whose name was Joseph, of the house of David; and the virgin's name was Mary. And the angel came in unto her, and said, Hail, thou that art highly favored, the Lord is with thee: blessed art thou among women.*
And when she saw him, she was troubled at his saying, and cast in her mind what manner of salutation this should be.
And the angel said unto her, Fear not, Mary: for thou hast found favor with God. And, behold, thou shalt conceive in thy womb, and bring forth a son, and shalt call his name Yeshua."

- Therefore, Yeshua would have been conceived six months after Sivan 20, around the month of Kislev, about the time of Hanukkah. He was the "Light of the World", conceived during the Festival of Lights!

- Traveling on to Bethlehem, the wise men found the child and His parents in a house (Matthew 2:11); whereas in the Luke account, the shepherds found Him in a stable (Luke 2:7, 16).
- There is no discrepancy between these two accounts, for likely the new mother and child were moved from the stable following the birth. The fact that He was born in a stable is a clue to the time of His birth, for in Hebrew, a stable is called a "sukkah" (Genesis 33:17).
- "Sukkot" (the name of the festival) is the plural form of sukkah.
- Joseph and Miriam (Mary) bring the child into JerUSAlem 40 days after Yeshua's birth. This indicates that Herod died within this same 40 days. The chronology of these 40 days is imperative in correctly finding Yeshua's birth date.
- The most likely scenario is this: Joseph and Miriam (Mary) come to Jerusalem for the Festival of Sukkot (September or October), planning to stay in the nearby Bethlehem in order to register for the census. Unable to find a room at the inn, they are given shelter in a stable, which just happens to be a sukkah.
- During the night, the wise men arrive in JerUSAlem and speak to Herod.

The Mark of the Feasts!

- Meanwhile, Mary gives birth. The heavenly host appear to the shepherds, proclaiming the Messiah has been born. They go to pay Him homage in the stable, while the wise men are making their way to Bethlehem. The shepherds leave to "noise it abroad", and Mary is moved to a house. The wise men arrive and during the night, are warned by God concerning Herod. Joseph and Mary take the child and flee to Egypt. There they remain until they are told by God that Herod is dead. On returning to Judea, they dedicate Yeshua according to the Law, receiving the prophecies of Anna and Simeon.

- It is apparent that as long as Herod was alive, they could not appear at the Temple. Therefore, if the approximate date of Herod's death could be determined, it would establish the season of Yeshua's birth. The Jewish historian, Josephus (who lived during the first century), documents in detail Herod's death.

- Josephus relates that Herod became very ill immediately following an act of impiety against the priesthood, at which time an eclipse of the moon occurred. This eclipse, the only one mentioned by Josephus, happened March 13th in the year of the Julian period 4710, and the fourth year before the Common Era.

- Herod's illness lasted several months and is documented in great detail as being "painful and distressful". Many times, cures were sought and brought about temporary relief; however, nothing prevented imminent death.
- According to Josephus' calculations, Herod's death occurred about September, in the fourth year before the Common Era.
- Therefore, with the knowledge that Herod died in autumn, the same time of year as Sukkot, and that his death was within 40 days of the birth of Yeshua, it is established that Yeshua was born at this time of year.

The Mark of the Feasts!

*"And it was at Jerusalem, the Feast of Dedication…
and Yeshua walked in the temple!"*
John 10:22-23

Angel Mariah

Feasts of Dedication - Hanukkah
Hebrew: Hanukkah (Festival of Lights)

"And it was at JerUSAlem the Feasts of the Dedication, and it was winter. And Yeshua walked in the temple in Solomon's porch"
(John 10:22-23).

General Notes:
- Hanukkah (also spelled Chanukah) is the Hebrew word for "dedication".
- It refers to the celebration of re-dedicating the Temple on 25 Kislev, 165 B.C., after it had been desecrated by the Syrian King Antiochus Epiphanes.
- The Hanukkah story preserves the epic struggle and the heroic exploits of one of the greatest Jewish victories of all time and their independence from Greco-Syrian oppression.

What is Hanukkah:
- Hanukkah is an eight-day feast celebration which occurs during the beginning of Winter.
- On the Hebrew calendar, it is celebrated beginning on the 25th day of Kislev, the ninth Hebrew month, which corresponds roughly to the Christmas season in December.

The Mark of the Feasts!

- The holiday begins only 75 days after Yom Kippur or 'The Day of Atonement'.

The Meaning of Hanukkah:

- The "400 Silent Years" refers to the period between the closing of the Tanakh (Hebrew word for '1st Testament') and the writings of the 2nd Testament.
- This period is called the "400 Silent Years" because during that time, God gave no new revelation to His people. From Malachi to John the Baptist, the prophetic voice in Israel was silent. There were no prophets, no visions, and no angelic visits.
- Many significant events in Israel's history occurred during these four centuries: the development of the Synagogue, the rise of the Sadducees and Pharisees, and the domination by Rome.
- Hanukkah (or the "Feast of Dedication") — perhaps the most important of the events — also took place during these "400 Silent Years".
- Hanukkah is not mentioned in the Tanakh (1st Testament) but it does appear once in the New Testament Gospel of John. During Yeshua's lifetime, Hanukkah had become a regular holiday (Jn. 10:22-23).

- You read about the story of Hanukkah in the books of 1 and 2 Maccabees. The Books of Maccabee are among the 14 books of the Old Testament Apocrypha, a collection of non-inspired Jewish writings written between 200 B.C. and A.D. 100. Although Jews and Protestant Christians do not consider these books a part of the Torah, they are, however, a valuable historical record.

- Hanukkah is actually a relatively minor holiday on the Jewish calendar and yet, it is the best known among American non-Jews, perhaps because the date often coincides with the Christmas season. It is a relatively new holiday, dating back only to 165 B.C., unlike Passover and Yom Kippur, which were Biblical holidays God gave to Moses at Sinai.

- When we read the story of Hanukkah and the Maccabees, it seems like the whole event takes place over a few weeks; the battles take place, the Jews win, and the Greeks go home! But, in fact, it takes 25 years of fighting with great casualties on both side.

- The celebration of Hanukkah was observed for 600 years before the "jar of oil" story first appeared in Jewish literature. The Maccabees recaptured and rededicated

The Mark of the Feasts!

the Temple in Jerusalem in 164 B.C. The history of the Maccabean revolt recorded in the Book of Maccabees written shortly after the revolt makes no mention of the miracle of the oil.

- The Talmud (Hebrew instruction/study — Judaism's holiest book (actually, a collection of books)) — states that when the Temple was being restored, there was enough oil found to last for only one day and yet, by some miraculous provision of God, the oil lasted for eight days — long enough for a new batch to be prepared.

Jewish Customs of Hanukkah in the Home:
- The most visible aspect of the observance of Hanukkah is lighting of the special Hanukkah Menorah (also called Hanukkiah).
- As opposed to the seven candlesticks of the Temple Menorah, the Hanukkiah (Hanukkah Menorah) holds eight candles (one for each night of Hanukkah).
- An additional place (usually in the center and lifted higher than the others) is reserved for the ninth candle, called the Shamash in Hebrew (Shamus in Yiddish), which means servant.

- The Shamash or servant candle is lit first and is always used to light the other candles, one for each of the eight days.
- Other than this, there are no restrictions on the shape of the Hanukkiah, so artists exercise a great deal of creativity in designing them.
- The candles are placed in the Hanukkiah from right to left and kindled from left to right.
- The light is supposed to be displayed prominently, in a window, etc. where all who pass by will see it and be reminded of the miracle of the "Light of the World".
- The Hanukkiah lights may not be used for any practical purposes; only for the celebration of the holiday.
- It is from this practice that Hanukkah derives its second name, "Festival of Lights".
- On the first night of Hanukkah, a specific blessing is to be read before lighting the Hanukkiah candles.
- For the remaining seven days, traditionally, other specific Hanukkah scripture readings are recited.
- Hanukkah is not considered sacred, so all work is allowed during the eight-day period except for the weekly Sabbath.

The Mark of the Feasts!

In Israel:

- On the eve of Hanukkah, marathon runners are sent to the village of Modin, the initial site of the ancient Maccabean revolt.
- Flaming freedom torches are lit from the Hanukkiah and are carried by the runners to Jerusalem.
- A procession is held at the Western Wall of the Temple to kindle the Great Menorah.
- This ceremony represents the freedom and the spirit of martyrdom which made this freedom possible.

A Time of Gifts, Treats, and Songs:

- Hanukkah is a time of gift-giving, especially in America, because of its proximity to the tradition of Christmas.
- At sundown, families gather to kindle the Hanukkiah (the Hanukkah Menorah) flames, rededicate themselves to their faith, and share in festive meals and the sharing of gifts.
- Some traditional Jewish homes give one Hanukkah gift at the end of the eight-day celebration while others give eight gifts — one gift for each of the eight days.
- Among the Ashkenazim (Jews of Eastern Europe), it is traditional to eat latkes (potato pancakes) and

applesauce. The latkes are fried in oil as a reminder of the miraculous oil.

- Sephardic Jews preserve the tradition of eating sufganiyot, a kind of deep-fried, jelly-filled doughnut without the hole, sprinkled with powdered sugar.
- Hanukkah is also a special time of the year for tzadekah (charity). Associated with the lights, special contributions are often given to charities for the blind.
- Hanukkah is also a time of singing.
- An Ashkenazic tradition is the singing of Maoz Tzur, or "Mighty Rock", which takes its name from Isaiah 26:4.
- A popular Sephardic tradition is the reciting of Psalm 30.

A Time of Games — The Dreidel Tradition:

- The dreidel is a four-sided top with one of the Hebrew letters — Num, Gimel, Heh, and Shin — on each side.
- These letters stand for the phrase "Nes Gadol Hayah Sham" (translated: A Great Miracle Happened There). In Israel, the last word is changed to "here" since it was in Israel that the miracle of Hanukkah occurred.
- The letters also stand for the instructions to a game which is played with the top, and so it is said that the dreidel was used as a teaching tool in disguise because in times and places where the Jewish people were

forbidden to teach their religion to the children, the dreidel could be passed off as an innocent toy.
- It is said that the Jewish children of Judea during the Maccabean period wanted to study the Torah, but it was forbidden. They came up with a creative answer: They would study the scrolls in the streets until a foreign soldier came. Then, they would quickly hide the scroll, bring out the dreidels, and pretend to be engrossed in an innocent game of tops! The soldiers left and the Torah study would begin again.
- Children get "Hanukkah-Gelt" (Hanukkah Money) which is usually foil-covered chocolate coins from parents and grandparents. These coins are used to wager with and make the dreidel game more interesting.
- This tradition is preserved primarily from Eastern Europe.

CONCLUSION

So, there you have it—a microscopic look into God's appointed times, His Holy Days...The **FEASTS** of the **LORD**!

God preordained these appointments in accordance to the **GREATEST** commandments, repeated three times a day by Orthodox Jews, known as the Shemah:

"Hear, oh Israel... You shall love the Lord thy God with all your heart, soul, and mind!"

The Jewish economy is rich in beauty and spiritual lessons. By honoring these holy times, we come closer to God in our relationship with Him. These Holy Days gift us with a more in-depth look into the **character of God**, **His timing**, **His preciseness**, and (above all), **His beauty!**

When Yeshua was on the earth, He, too, lived according to the instructions in the Torah to honor these Feasts Days. Yeshua highlighted this blessing in Luke 10:27 when He said, *"Love God with all your heart, soul, and mind; and the second is like unto it, 'Love your neighbor as yourself'"*.

These Feasts Days not only provide insight into the character of God; they also provide a wonderful opportunity for God's people to unite, celebrate, and have fun together!

The Mark of the Feasts!

Yeshua further highlighted these instructions according to Deuteronomy 14:29 when He repeated the instruction God gave Israel through Moses that "*the stranger and the fatherless and the widow, which are within thy gates, shall come and shall eat and be satisfied*".

These celebrations taught the joy of true hospitality. The people were cared for throughout the year, even the bereaved and the poor. The spiritual blessings given to Israel were not for themselves. These Feasts Days have a wider lesson: God gave the *Bread of Life* to them that they might break it unto the world... the center of JerUSAlem.

It is the author's prayer that this book will bless you and your family. May it serve as your divine appointment.

ABOUT THE AUTHOR

Angel Mariah earned her Doctor of Naturopathy Degree in 1997, where she studied natural therapies, herbs, detoxification programs, and colon hydrotherapy. For over 20 years, she owned and operated a natural health and wellness center in Santa Barbara, California.

She's worked with clients from around the world, detoxing their body, mind, and spirit back to its original state of wholeness and wellbeing, using all-natural therapies such as diet, detoxification programs, and healthy lifestyle choices.

Becoming a natural doctor was the culmination of her lifelong interest in the function of disease on the physical as well as the spiritual body.

The Mark of the Feasts!

As a Christian, she has studied the Bible in depth and believes that the honor of God's "*7 divine appointments*" personally transformed her life into a more youthful body, mind, and spirit!

She also believes that the Feasts of the LORD are a key, a hidden "*right of passage*", that connects our individual and collective souls to who we are as **ONE!**

Shemah Yisrael!

BIBLIOGRAPHY

Chabad Staff. *Holidays: Jewish New Year. How to Build a Sukkah.* Retrieved August 17, 2017 from http://www.chabad.org/holidays/JewishNewYear/template_cdo/aid/420823/jewish/How-to-Build-a-Sukka.htm

Chumney, E. (1999). *Restoring the Two Houses of Israel.* Serenity Books, Hagerstown, MD.

Coulter, R. (2003). *God's Plan for Mankind Revealed by His Sabbath and Holy Days.* York Publishing Company, Hollister, CA.

Drake, M. and Drake, R. (2005). *God's Holidays.* Bible Explorations, Terra Bella, CA.

Howard, K. and Rosenthal, M. (1997). *The Feasts of the LORD.* Thomas Nelson Publishing, Nashville, TN.

Manfredine, S. (2004). *The Testimony of the Moon.* Lighted Way Publishing, CA.

Martins, R. (n.d.) *Fun Facts About the Bible You Never Knew.* Barbour Publishing, Uhrichsville, OH.

Sampson, R. and Pierce, L. (1999). *A Family Guide to the Bible Holidays*. Heart of Wisdom Publishing, Stafford, VA.

Wootten, B.R. (2001). *Who is Israel? A Study Guide*. Key of David Publishing, St. Cloud, FL.

Wootten, B.R. (2002). *Israel's Feasts and Their Fullness*. Key of David Publishing, St. Cloud, FL.

NOTES

The Mark of the Feasts!

Angel Mariah

The Mark of the Feasts!

Angel Mariah

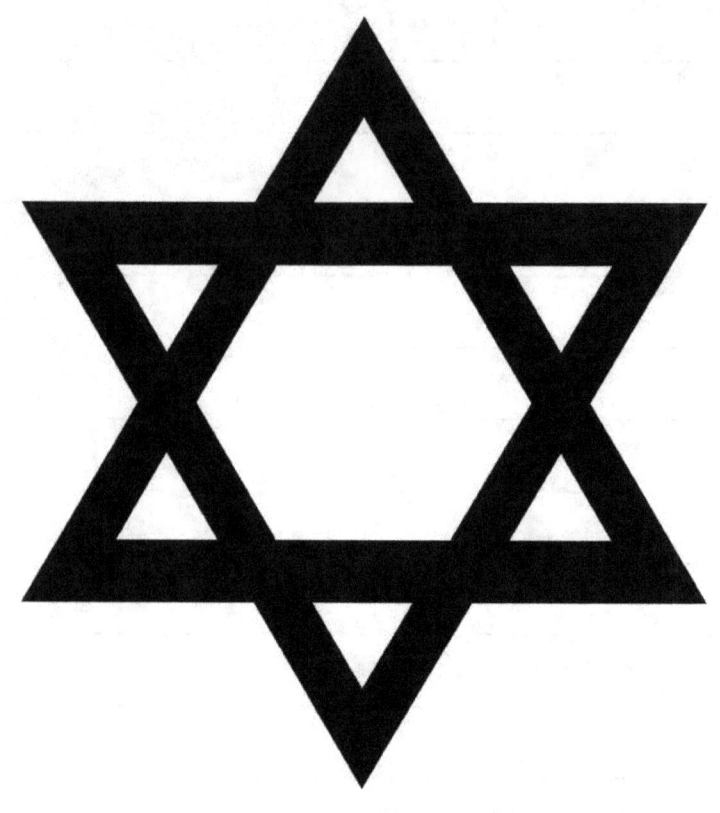

Shomer Doltot Yisrael!
שומר דלתות ישראל

www.ingramcontent.com/pod-product-compliance
Lightning Source LLC
Chambersburg PA
CBHW070108120526
44588CB00032B/1382